PANORAMA

BUILDING PERSPECTIVE THROUGH READING

KATHLEEN F. FLYNN

DAPHNE MACKEY

LATRICIA TRITES

with DENA DANIEL and ADRIANNE OCHOA

OXFORD

UNIVERSITY PRESS

OXFORD
UNIVERSITY PRESS

198 Madison Avenue
New York, NY 10016 USA

Great Clarendon Street, Oxford OX2 6DP UK

Oxford University Press is a department of the University of Oxford.
It furthers the University's objective of excellence in research, scholarship,
and education by publishing worldwide in

Oxford New York

Auckland Cape Town Dar es Salaam Hong Kong Karachi
Kuala Lumpur Madrid Melbourne Mexico City Nairobi
New Delhi Shanghai Taipei Toronto

With offices in

Argentina Austria Brazil Chile Czech Republic France Greece
Guatemala Hungary Italy Japan Poland Portugal Singapore
South Korea Switzerland Thailand Turkey Ukraine Vietnam

OXFORD and OXFORD ENGLISH are registered trademarks of
Oxford University Press

Developer: Angela M. Castro, English Language Trainers
Executive Publisher: Janet Aitchison
Editor: Phebe W. Szatmari
Art Director: Maj Hagsted
Senior Designer: Mia Gomez
Art Editor: Robin Fadool
Production Manager: Shanta Persaud
Production Controller: Eve Wong

ISBN-13: 978 0 19 430543 3
ISBN-10: 0 19 430543 0

10 9 8 7 6 5 4 3 2 1

Printed in Hong Kong.

Acknowledgments:

Cover art:
Hans Hofmann
Combinable Wall I and II
1961
Oil on canvas
Overall: 84-1/2 x 112-1/2 inches
University of California, Berkeley Art Museum; Gift of the artist.

The publisher would like to thank the following for their permission to
reproduce photographs: Georgia O'Keefe near Pink House Courtesy Museum
of New Mexico, Neg. Number 9763, v; *Red Poppy 1971* © 2005 The Georgia
O'Keefe Foundation/Artists Rights Society (ARS), New York, v; Ronald C. Saari;
Nighthawks, by Edward Hopper, photography by Robert Hashimoto. Photography
© The Art Institute of Chicago, 2; Ronald C. Saari, 4; Ronald C. Saari, 6; *Wizard
of Oz*, Courtesy Photofest; *Gone with the Wind*, Courtesy Everett Collection, 11;
Courtesy Everett Collection, 12; *Bride and Prejudice*, Miramax Everett Collection
Courtesy Everett Collection, 14; Globe Photos, Fitzroy Barrett, 16; Index Stock
Imagery, Inc.: Barry M. Winiker, 21; Index Stock Imagery, Inc.: Stewart Cohen,
21; Courtesy of the President's Council on Physical Fitness and Sports, 22; Index
Stock Imagery, Inc.: Mark Hunt, 24; Index Stock Imagery, Inc., 26; Courtesy
Library of Congress, Geography and Map Division, 31; Public Domain/San
Francisco Museum, 32; Index Stock Imagery, Inc.: Dave Bartruff, 34; Alamy: J.C.
Leacock, 36; *Haida Totems, Cha-atl, Queen Charlotte Island*, Courtesy British Columbia
Archives, Call Number PDP00612, 41; Courtesy British Columbia Archives,
Call Number D-03843, 42; LifeinKorea.com, 44; John and Carolyn Smyly, 46;
Hearst Castle®/CA State Parks, 51; Julia Morgan Collection, Special Collections,
California Polytechnic State University, 52; Hearst Castle®/CA State Parks, 54;
Hearst Castle®/CA State Parks, 56; Index Stock Imagery, Inc.: Barry M. Winiker,
61; The Granger Collection, 62 (Edward Cope); Peabody Museum of Natural
History, 62 (Othniel Charles Marsh); age footstock/SuperStock, 64; Philip James
Corwin/CORBIS, 66; Courtesy Apple, Inc., 71; © New York Newswire/CORBIS:
Steve Sands, 72; Index Stock Imagery, Inc.: David Ball, 74

The authors and publisher would like to acknowledge the following individuals
for their invaluable input during the development of this series:
Russell Frank, Pasadena City College, CA; Virginia Heringer, Pasadena City
College, CA; Barbara Howard, Daly Community College, IL; Maydell Jenks, Katy
Independent School District, TX; JoShell Koliva, Newcomer School, Ontario, CA;
Kathy Krokar, Truman Community College, IL; Catherine Slawson; University of
California, Davis, CA; Laura Walsh; City College of San Francisco, CA

CONTENTS

TO THE TEACHER   iv

ESSENTIAL READING SKILLS   v

UNIT 1   AMERICAN CULTURE: DINERS   1
Chapter 1 Edward Hopper: American Artist   2
Chapter 2 Diners   4
Chapter 3 Saving a Piece of America   6

UNIT 2   FILM STUDIES: THE ENTERTAINMENT INDUSTRY   11
Chapter 1 Carole Lombard: Actress   12
Chapter 2 Bollywood   14
Chapter 3 Star-Making   16

UNIT 3   PSYCHOLOGY: THE MIND-BODY CONNECTION   21
Chapter 1 Denise Austin: Fitness Expert   22
Chapter 2 Bridal Boot Camp   24
Chapter 3 Competition Yoga   26

UNIT 4   U.S. HISTORY: THE OLD WEST   31
Chapter 1 The Legend of Black Bart   32
Chapter 2 The California Gold Rush   34
Chapter 3 The Pony Express   36

UNIT 5   ANTHROPOLOGY: TOTEM POLES   41
Chapter 1 Emily Carr: Painter of Totem Poles   42
Chapter 2 *Jangseung:* Totem Poles in Korea   44
Chapter 3 History Speaks: What Does a Totem Pole Say?   46

UNIT 6   ARCHITECTURE: VISUAL ART   51
Chapter 1 Julia Morgan: Architect   52
Chapter 2 Hearst Castle   54
Chapter 3 The Problem at Hearst Castle   56

UNIT 7   NATURAL HISTORY: ANIMALS OF THE PAST   61
Chapter 1 Marsh and Cope: The Bone Wars   62
Chapter 2 The Morrison Formation of Colorado   64
Chapter 3 Hunting for Fossils in Los Angeles   66

UNIT 8   TECHNOLOGY: COMPUTERS AND THE INTERNET   71
Chapter 1 Steve Jobs: Modern Inventor   72
Chapter 2 The New Silicon Valley   74
Chapter 3 Technology Changes Our Lives   76

Essential Reading Skills: Answer Key and Explanations   81

Vocabulary Index   84

Common Irregular Verbs   86

TO THE TEACHER

Welcome to *Panorama 1*, a reading skills text for beginning level students. *Panorama 1* combines high-interest reading passages from the content areas with a strong vocabulary strand and extensive reading skills practice to prepare students for the challenges of academic reading.

Each of the eight main units consists of three chapters, and each chapter has a thematically-linked reading passage. The first passage is about a person, the second about a related place, and the third about a related concept or event.

The book begins with an introductory unit, **Essential Reading Skills**, that presents and practices the core reading skills needed for academic success.

WHAT IS IN EACH UNIT?

Before You Read

This opening page introduces the theme of the unit. The questions and photographs can be used to activate students' prior knowledge and stimulate discussion before reading.

Prepare to Read

This section introduces the topic of the chapter. The questions and photographs encourage students to become engaged in the topic while sharing their own thoughts and experiences.

Word Focus

This matching activity introduces students to new or unfamiliar words that they will see in the reading passage. Students match the ten words with simple definitions.

Scan

This activity encourages students to make a prediction about a specific piece of information that appears in the passage. The aim is to motivate students to read the passages quickly as they try to find the answer.

Reading Passage

Each reading in Book 1 is about 225 words. The language is carefully graded using the Fry Readability Scale so that students gain confidence in reading; the average Fry Readability Score in *Panorama 1* is 5.0.

Check Your Comprehension

These multiple-choice questions check students' understanding of the passage. The questions include key skills such as understanding the main idea, reading for details, and reading for inference.

Vocabulary Review

This section reviews the vocabulary presented in the unit. It includes a wide variety of activities, such as **Words in Context** (filling in the gaps), **Which Meaning?** (choosing the definition that fits), **Wrong Word** (finding the word that doesn't fit the group), **Word Families** (choosing the part of speech that fits), and **Crossword Puzzles**. These activities help students use the new words as part of their active vocabulary.

Wrap It Up

This final section of the unit gives students the opportunity to discuss the theme of the unit with more confidence and holistic understanding. The last activity asks students to respond in writing about the passage they enjoyed the most. This activity reinforces what students have learned about the unit's theme.

The Essential Reading Skills: Answer Key and Explanations, a Vocabulary Index, and a list of Common Irregular Verbs can be found at the back of the book for easy reference.

An *Answer Key* and *Assessment CD-ROM with ExamView® Test Generator* are available for use with *Panorama 1.*

ESSENTIAL READING SKILLS

▲ Georgia O'Keefe, 1887–1986

▲ Red Poppy 1971

PREVIEW AND PREDICT

Before you read, **preview** and **predict**. When you **preview**, you look at the photographs and the parts of a passage. When you **predict**, you make logical guesses about content.

A. Look at the photographs only. (Don't read the captions yet.) Answer these questions.

1. Describe what you see. _____
_____

2. Are the photographs old or new? How do you know? _____

_____

3. What can you guess, or **predict**, about the passage from the photographs? _____

B. Now read the captions. Answer these questions.

1. What information do these captions tell you? _____

_____

2. Is Georgia O'Keefe still living? How do you know? _____

_____

3. Have you heard of her or seen this painting? _____

_____

✔ Look at page 81 for the explanations.

Georgia O'Keefe: The Art of Nature

Georgia O'Keefe was a **pioneer** in the American art world. In the early 20th century, or 1900s, many women artists painted **portraits**, often of children
5 or of mothers with young children. Other women artists went into the **countryside** and painted **landscapes**. O'Keefe didn't paint **traditional** portraits or landscapes.

10 O'Keefe saw things differently. She saw a flower and painted its energy. Sometimes her whole **canvas** was just one flower. You can feel the energy of the flower. You view the painting like a small
15 insect, perhaps a bee or a butterfly. You see the inside of the flower. You feel the flower's soft **petals**. You see its bright colors. You can almost smell it.

Later, visits to New Mexico gave
20 O'Keefe new ideas for paintings. In the desert of New Mexico everything is dry.

Her paintings of the desert look dry like the desert. They have the colors of the desert. O'Keefe painted the big sky and
25 the red hills. Some of her paintings were very large.

One famous painting was the **skull** of a cow. You see the white bones and the blue sky. You can feel how dry, how arid,
30 the desert is. O'Keefe studied *notan*, a Japanese painting style. It uses light and dark colors. You see a light **image** and a darker **background**.

O'Keefe painted for more than 70
35 years. She died in 1986 at age 98. She created hundreds of pieces of art. Her large, colorful flowers and her paintings of the desert are still popular today. They appear on calendars and cards. Many
40 people have posters or prints of her paintings on their walls.

C. Read the title. Answer these questions.

1. Is the passage about a person, a place, or a thing? _____

2. What is the connection between the title and the photographs on page v? _____

3. What do you **predict** the passage will be about? _____

_____

D. Preview the passage. Look for words with special markings. Answer these questions.

1. How many words do you see in **boldface**? _____

2. How many words do you see in *italics*? _____

E. Look at the paragraphs. Answer these questions.

1. Which paragraph is the introduction? _____

2. Which paragraph is the conclusion? _____

✔ Look at page 81 for the explanations.

SKIMMING AND SCANNING

Sometimes, you need to read quickly to look for certain information. This is called **skimming** and **scanning**. You **skim** when you read quickly. As you **skim**, your eyes **scan** for specific information. Use the passage and these questions to practice.

A. To skim, let your eyes move quickly over the passage. Answer these questions by writing *Yes* or *No*.

Does it have dialogue? _____

Is it a story? _____

Does it have technical vocabulary? _____

Does it have charts and diagrams? _____

Is it academic or professional? _____

Does it have dates and events in a person's life? _____

Is it a biography? _____

B. Before you scan, decide what to look for. Find an example of each of these.

1. a word in **boldface** _____

2. a word in *italics* _____

3. a date _____

4. a number _____

5. a place name _____

6. a person's name _____

✔ Look at page 81 for the explanations.

C. Now answer this question.

Guess if this is true or false. Circle *a* or *b*.

Georgia O'Keefe painted for 98 years.

a. True　　**b.** False

Scan the passage quickly to check your answer.

✔ Look at page 81 for the explanation.

MAIN IDEA

Every passage has a **main idea**. This is the most important topic or most general idea. Each paragraph also has a **main idea**. It is often in the first sentence, but not always.

D. Read the passage and answer the question. Circle your answer.

1. What is the main topic of the passage?
   A. a painting of a flower
   B. a famous woman artist
   C. a Japanese style of painting
   D. art in the 1900s

✔ Look at page 82 for the explanation.

DETAIL

Every passage has many smaller, specific pieces of information that tell you more about the main idea. These are called **details**.

E. Read the passage and answer the questions. Circle your answers.

2. In the early 1900s, women artists often painted
   A. children
   B. women
   C. landscapes
   D. all of the above

3. O'Keefe painted the desert of
   A. New Mexico
   B. New York
   C. New Hampshire
   D. New Brunswick

4. What did O'Keefe paint?
   A. trees and butterflies
   B. flowers and bones
   C. rivers and lakes
   D. mothers and babies

✔ Look at page 82 for the explanations.

INFERENCE

You can use details to make logical guesses. These logical guesses are called **inferences**. Often you have to think about information in different parts of the passage and then piece the information together.

F. Read the passage and answer the questions. Circle your answers.

5. Which of the following is **not** true?
   A. People like O'Keefe's work.
   B. O'Keefe lived a long life.
   C. The flower paintings seem real.
   D. O'Keefe taught *notan* classes.

6. What can we say about O'Keefe?
   A. She loved nature.
   B. Her desert paintings all had flowers.
   C. Her paintings had birds and insects.
   D. She only used black and white paint.

✔ Look at page 83 for the explanations.

WORDS IN CONTEXT, PART 1

In every passage, you will often find words that are unfamiliar to you. Look for clues in the sentence or in nearby sentences to help you understand **words in context**.

G. Circle the answers with the same meaning as the words in boldface. Then underline the clues that helped you.

1. In the early 1900s, many women artists painted **portraits**, often of children or of mothers with young children.
   A. paintings of people
   B. paintings of animals
   C. paintings of trees and flowers

2. You see the inside of the flower. You feel the flower's soft **petals**. You see its bright colors.
   A. the colored part of a flower
   B. the leaves of the flower
   C. the stem of the flower

3. One famous painting was the **skull** of a cow. You see white bones and the blue sky.
   A. the blue color in the sky
   B. a white cow
   C. the bones of the head

WORDS IN CONTEXT, PART 2

Sometimes the author gives a clue by defining **words in context**. The author might include a definition, an example, or a synonym. Sometimes the author defines a foreign word. Commas often set off definitions in context.

4. Underline the part of the sentence that helps define *desert*.
   In the desert of New Mexico everything is dry.

5. Underline the two examples of insects. Circle the comma.
   You view the painting like a small insect, perhaps a bee or a butterfly.

6. Underline the synonyms in this sentence.
   You can feel how dry, how arid, the desert is.

7. Underline the definition of the foreign word *notan*. Circle the comma.
   O'Keefe studied *notan,* a Japanese painting style.

✔ Look at page 83 for the explanations.

AMERICAN CULTURE

DINERS

▲ The Salem Diner in Salem, Massachusetts

▲ The Empire Diner in New York City

BEFORE YOU READ

Answer these questions.

1. What is your favorite restaurant?

2. Look at the photos. Describe these restaurants.

3. Have you ever eaten in a restaurant like these? Would you like to?

CHAPTER 1

Nighthawks by Edward Hopper, 1942, The Art Institute of Chicago

PREPARE TO READ

Discuss these questions.

1. What do you see in this painting by Edward Hopper?
2. How does this painting make you feel?

WORD FOCUS

Match the words with their definitions.

A.

1. community ___
2. connected ___
3. diner ___
4. emotion ___
5. empty ___

   a. associated; related
   b. a strong feeling such as love, anger, or fear
   c. having nothing or nobody inside
   d. a group of people who have something in common
   e. a restaurant that serves simple, cheap food in an informal atmosphere

B.

1. image ___
2. lit up ___
3. loneliness ___
4. realist ___
5. sense ___

   a. the feeling from something
   b. unhappiness when someone is not with other people
   c. having light
   d. a picture or description in a book, movie, or painting
   e. a person who sees things as they really are

SCAN

Guess if this is true or false. Circle *a* or *b*.

Edward Hopper painted only diners.

a. True   **b.** False

Scan the passage quickly to check your answer.

Edward Hopper: American Artist

The most famous **diner** in America isn't a real place. It is an **image** in a painting by Edward Hopper.

Hopper was different from many 5 artists of the early 1900s. He was a **realist**. He painted everyday things such as a diner or a gas station. You may ask, "Why would anyone buy a painting of a gas station?" But Hopper's paintings 10 show more than just buildings and people. They show the **loneliness** of life, an **emotion** that Hopper felt very strongly himself. He once said, "I don't think I ever tried to paint the American 15 scene; I'm trying to paint myself."

Hopper's paintings show feelings that many people felt in the 1900s. This was a time of great change. Many people were moving into the cities from farms 20 and small towns. These new arrivals missed the **sense** of **community** they had in their small towns. The big cities, with their tall buildings and so many strangers, seemed frightening to many 25 people.

Hopper's painting of the diner is called *Nighthawks*. It is a realistic **image** of buildings and people. The diner is **lit up**, but it doesn't seem warm and 30 welcoming. The people inside don't seem happy or **connected** to each other. The city outside looks dark and **empty**. This is how Edward Hopper saw the city. This is how Edward Hopper saw 35 life.

CHECK YOUR COMPREHENSION

Read the passage again and answer the questions. Circle your answers.

MAIN IDEA
1. What is the main topic of the passage?
   A. a painting of a diner
   B. an artist who painted a diner
   C. the time when diners were popular
   D. a diner in a big city

DETAIL
2. What did Hopper do for a living?
   A. He owned gas stations.
   B. He was an artist.
   C. He worked in a diner.
   D. He was a farmer.

3. What did Hopper paint?
   A. small-town communities
   B. realistic images of America
   C. famous people
   D. warm scenes of American life

4. Why was Hopper called a realist?
   A. He painted things the way they looked.
   B. His paintings were not like real life.
   C. He painted art for magazines and newspapers.
   D. He painted himself.

INFERENCE
5. Most artists in the early 1900s painted
   A. realistic images
   B. modern buildings
   C. images that were not true to life
   D. people in cities

6. People like Hopper's paintings because
   A. the paintings don't look real
   B. they feel happy when they look at the paintings
   C. they like gas stations and diners
   D. the paintings show a lot of feeling

CHAPTER 2

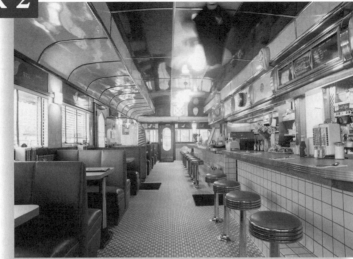

◀ Inside a typical diner

PREPARE TO READ

Discuss these questions.

1. Describe the restaurant in the picture.

2. How do you think it looks?

WORD FOCUS

Match the words with their definitions.

A.
1. booth ___   **a.** a person who buys something
2. copy ___   **b.** a company that makes things
3. counter ___   **c.** imitate; do the same as somebody else
4. customer ___   **d.** a long, flat surface like a table
5. manufacturer ___   **e.** a long seat and a table attached to a wall

B.
1. popularity ___   **a.** not difficult or complicated
2. serve ___   **b.** the quality of being liked by many people
3. simple ___   **c.** a seat that does not have a back or arms
4. stool ___   **d.** a vehicle with four wheels that is pulled by a horse
5. wagon ___   **e.** give food or drinks to someone during a meal

SCAN

Guess the answer. Circle *a* or *b*.

Where did the name *diners* come from?

a. train cars   **b.** people who are eating

Scan the passage quickly to check your answer.

Diners

Do you like to eat at fast-food restaurants? Before McDonald's® or KFC®, there were diners. There is nothing fancy about a diner. Diners have **simple**,
5 inexpensive food. They **serve** breakfast all day. Of course, there are no tablecloths!

How did diners start? The first diner was a lunch **wagon**. In the 1800s, Walter Scott had a horse and cart in
10 Providence, Rhode Island. He sold lunch to people from his cart. Eventually, he added a roof to the cart to keep his **customers** dry.

Many people copied Scott's idea.
15 Companies began to make special carts. The carts had **counters** and **stools**. Not everyone had enough money to buy these special carts, so they built their own from old streetcars.
20 Not everyone liked these eating places. Some were dirty and not very comfortable. So the companies made some changes. They made the carts longer. They added **booths** and tables.
25 But the biggest change came because of trains. Trains started to serve meals in special dining cars. These dining cars were very popular. **Manufacturers** began to **copy** the style of train cars. The
30 companies called their new food cars "diners."

The new diners were a hit. In the late 1940s, 12 manufacturers made diners. The manufacturers sold them complete
35 with dishes, pots, and pans. People could order one and start their own business!

In the 1960s, diners lost **popularity** to fast-food restaurants. Today, only about two thousand diners remain in the
40 United States.

CHECK YOUR COMPREHENSION

Read the passage again and answer the questions. Circle your answers.

MAIN IDEA

1. What is the main topic of the passage?
   A. big restaurants
   B. starting a restaurant
   C. a special type of restaurant
   D. the way diners are built

DETAIL

2. Walter Scott's lunch wagon had
   A. places to sit
   B. a counter
   C. a roof
   D. tables

3. What did manufacturers add to lunch wagons first?
   A. places to sit and eat
   B. windows
   C. booths
   D. special foods

4. Why did manufacturers copy train cars?
   A. They were very popular.
   B. They were easy to build.
   C. They were bigger than diners.
   D. They were not expensive.

INFERENCE

5. Diners were popular because
   A. of the price and quality of their food
   B. people didn't have pots and pans
   C. there were no restaurants
   D. people like stools better than chairs

6. When were diners most popular?
   A. in the 1800s
   B. in the early 1900s
   C. in the 1940s
   D. in the 1960s

CHAPTER 3

Mickey's Diner in
St. Paul, Minnesota

PREPARE TO READ

Discuss these questions.

1. What buildings do you think are beautiful?

2. What do you think of the diner in the photo?

WORD FOCUS

Match the words with their definitions.

A.

1. architecture ___   **a.** close because there is no more money

2. design ___   **b.** a series of things that are written one after another

3. efficient ___   **c.** the style or design of buildings

4. go out of business ___   **d.** able to work well

5. list ___   **e.** the way something is planned or made

B.

1. modern ___   **a.** fashionable

2. sleek ___   **b.** destroy a building

3. surround ___   **c.** having an elegant, smooth shape

4. tear down ___   **d.** of the present time

5. trendy ___   **e.** be all around something

SCAN

Guess if this is true or false. Circle *a* or *b*.

Some diners are important historical buildings.

a. True   **b.** False

Scan the passage quickly to check your answer.

Saving a Piece of America

A shiny, old silver diner called Mickey's sits in the center of St. Paul, Minnesota. Tall, **modern** office buildings **surround** it. You see it and
5 wonder, "Why is that diner still here?"

Mickey's Diner is on the National Register. This is a **list** of important historic buildings in the United States. Because of their importance, no one can
10 **tear down** these buildings. So now you ask, "But a diner? What's so important about an old diner?"

True, diners do look strange. This is what makes them special. Their
15 **architecture** is very unusual. Their **design** was very modern for the time. Diners used new materials like steel and plastic. They were **efficient** and **sleek**.

Diners are also historical. They
20 represent a time when trains were fashionable. They show the change from small town to modern city. They also show people's interest in the future.

In a way, diners were too **trendy**.
25 They soon began to look old. In the 1960s and 1970s, other fast-food restaurants became more popular than diners. Many diners **went out of business**. Now only a few diners
30 remain.

Some people want to save diners because they are part of the American past. Other people think diners are ugly. These people say, "Save them in a
35 museum. Don't keep them in downtown St. Paul!"

CHECK YOUR COMPREHENSION

Read the passage again and answer the questions. Circle your answers.

MAIN IDEA
1. What is the main topic of the passage?
   A. why people like diners
   B. Mickey's Diner
   C. the historical value of diners
   D. the strange way diners look

DETAIL
2. What is the National Register?
   A. a list of modern buildings
   B. a list of all the old buildings in St. Paul
   C. a list of buildings that no one can tear down
   D. a list of all the diners in the U.S.

3. When diners were made
   A. they seemed very modern
   B. they were too trendy
   C. they weren't strange looking
   D. they weren't as popular as fast-food restaurants

4. When did diners start to go out of business?
   A. in the late 1800s
   B. in the early 1900s
   C. in the second half of the last century
   D. in this century

INFERENCE
5. Mickey's Diner
   A. is the only diner left
   B. is popular with everyone
   C. is in a museum
   D. is a historic building

6. Which of these statements is true?
   A. Diners no longer serve simple food.
   B. It is important to preserve unique architecture.
   C. They tore down Mickey's.
   D. Trains are the cool way to travel.

VOCABULARY REVIEW

From Chapter 1: *Edward Hopper: American Artist*

1. What does *miss* mean in this context?

> These new arrivals missed the sense of community they had in their small towns.

A. miss *(verb)* to arrive too late for something

B. miss *(verb)* to feel sad because somebody is not with you or because you do not have something you once had

C. miss *(noun)* a failure to hit, catch, or see something you were aiming at

From Chapter 2: *Diners*

2. What does *hit* mean in this context?

> The new diners were a hit.

A. hit *(verb)* to press something such as a button to operate a machine

B. hit *(verb)* to touch something or somebody with a lot of force

C. hit *(noun)* a person or thing that is very popular or successful

From Chapter 3: *Saving a Piece of America*

3. What does *still* mean in this context?

> You see it and wonder, "Why is that diner still here?"

A. still *(adjective)* without moving

B. still *(adverb)* continuing until now

C. still *(noun)* a single photograph that is taken from a scene in a movie

WRONG WORD

One word in each group does not fit. Circle the word.

1. booths	pans	stools	chairs
2. business	architecture	design	plans
3. fashionable	trendy	popular	ugly
4. house	wagon	cart	train
5. business	company	customer	manufacturer
6. loneliness	happiness	design	emotion

WORDS IN CONTEXT

Fill in the blanks with words from each box.

architecture	design	list	manufacturers	wagon

1. I like to walk around the city and look at the _____ .
2. Before I go to the grocery store, I always write a _____ of things that I need.
3. The _____ of that chair is beautiful, but it's not very comfortable to sit in.
4. Most of the _____ of diners went out of business in the 1960s.
5. He was smart to add a roof to the _____ . Then people didn't get wet when it rained.

popular	serve	simple	surround	trendy

6. Tall trees _____ the house. It's almost hidden.
7. She loves to shop and always wears very _____ clothes.
8. Fast-food restaurants became very _____ in the 1960s.
9. The food is nothing special. It's very _____ .
10. What time do they _____ breakfast?

community	efficient	emotions	lit up	modern

11. The city looks beautiful at night with all the buildings _____ .
12. It's not old-fashioned. It's very _____ .
13. Loneliness and anger are _____ .
14. People in the _____ were unhappy about plans to tear down the school.
15. She is not very _____ . It takes her a long time to get her work done.

WORD FAMILIES

Fill in the blanks with words from each box.

real *(adjective)*	reality *(noun)*	realist *(noun)*

1. He's a _____ . He's very logical about life.
2. These flowers are made of plastic. They're not _____ .

| connect *(verb)* | connected *(adjective)* | connection *(noun)* |

3. Where's the _____ between the two buildings?

4. They _____ on the first floor.

| manufacture *(verb)* | manufacturer *(noun)* | manufactured *(adjective)* |

5. The company used to _____ the diners in New York.

6. The _____ went out of business.

WRAP IT UP

DISCUSS THE THEME

Read these questions. Discuss your answers with a partner.

1. Why do people in the United States feel diners are special?

2. Should we save diners, or should we tear them down?

3. What can buildings from the past show us about society? Discuss examples such as schools, banks, libraries, and skyscrapers.

4. Which buildings in your city are old? What do they show about life in the past?

5. What buildings would you tear down in your neighborhood? In your city? Why?

RESPOND IN WRITING

Look back at the unit and choose the passage you enjoyed the most. Read it again. Why is this passage interesting? Write a few sentences.

_____

_____

_____

Now write one or two things you learned from the passage.

_____

_____

_____

FILM STUDIES
THE ENTERTAINMENT INDUSTRY

Gone with the Wind, 1939

The Wizard of Oz, 1939

BEFORE YOU READ

Answer these questions.

1. What kinds of movies do you like?

2. What was the last movie you saw? How did you like it?

3. What is your favorite movie?

CHAPTER 1

Carole Lombard and Clark Gable

PREPARE TO READ

Discuss these questions.

1. Who is your favorite movie actor or actress?

2. What is a silent movie? Have you ever seen one?

WORD FOCUS

Match the words with their definitions.

A.
1. accident ___   **a.** continue doing something
2. contract ___   **b.** well-known to many people
3. famous ___   **c.** a sudden event that causes damage
4. give up ___   **d.** stop doing something
5. keep on ___   **e.** a written legal agreement

B.
1. make-up ___   **a.** not using spoken words
2. scar ___   **b.** a place where movies are made
3. silent ___   **c.** a famous person in acting, music, or sports
4. star ___   **d.** a permanent mark on the skin from a cut
5. studio ___   **e.** things women put on the face to look more attractive

SCAN

Guess if this is true or false. Circle *a* or *b*.

Carole Lombard was married more than once.

a. True   **b.** False

Scan the passage quickly to check your answer.

Carole Lombard: Actress

Do you ever watch old movies? Maybe you will see one with Carole Lombard. She was a **famous** movie actress in the 1930s. She died when she
5 was only 34. In her short life she made 70 movies!

Lombard's real name was Jane Alice Peters. In 1921, she was playing baseball in the street near her home. A movie
10 director saw her and decided to put her in a movie. She was only 13 at the time. The movie was one of the last **silent** movies. At 16, she left school to act.

She got a **contract** in 1925 with a
15 film **studio**, 20th Century Fox. The studio gave her a new name, and she starred in several films. Then, at age 18, she was in a bad car **accident**.

The accident left **scars** on her face.
20 The studio ended her contract, but she did not **give up**. She wore a lot of **make-up**. She **kept on** acting.

It was Paramount Studio that made Lombard a **star**. She made many movies
25 for the studio. She also married two of their stars. Lombard was married to actor William Powell for only 23 months. But seven years later, she married the great love of her life, actor Clark Gable.
30 Gable played Rhett Butler in the movie *Gone with the Wind.*

Lombard was killed in a plane crash in 1942. Gable married again. But when he died, he was buried next to Lombard.
35 It was a great Hollywood love story.

CHECK YOUR COMPREHENSION

Read the passage again and answer the questions. Circle your answers.

MAIN IDEA

1. What is the main topic of the passage?
   A. silent movie stars
   B. one actress
   C. old film stars
   D. a love story

DETAIL

2. Why did 20th Century Fox end Carole Lombard's contract?
   A. because she was in an accident
   B. because she wasn't a good actress
   C. because she had scars on her face
   D. because she didn't want to work

3. When was Carole Lombard born?
   A. in 1908
   B. in 1911
   C. in 1918
   D. in 1921

4. How did Carole Lombard die?
   A. in a plane crash
   B. in a car accident
   C. during an operation
   D. of old age

INFERENCE

5. Lombard left school because
   A. school was too easy
   B. acting took all of her time
   C. her school closed
   D. her teachers didn't like her

6. Paramount hired Carole Lombard
   A. because she was in *Gone with the Wind*
   B. because she knew Clark Gable
   C. because she was a good actress
   D. because she had a contract

CHAPTER 2

Making a Bollywood movie

PREPARE TO READ

Discuss these questions.

1. Look at the photograph. What are the people's jobs?

2. Have you ever been to a movie studio? What did you see there?

WORD FOCUS

Match the words with their definitions.

A.
1. capital ___
2. early ___
3. film ___
4. industry ___
5. international ___

   a. near the beginning of a period of time
   b. involving other countries
   c. everything relating to a specific type business
   d. a movie
   e. the central place for an activity

B.
1. land ___
2. limited ___
3. nickname ___
4. perfect ___
5. recognize ___

   a. know something you have seen or heard before
   b. a piece of ground
   c. an informal name
   d. kept within a certain area
   e. as good as can be

SCAN

Guess the answer. Circle *a* or *b*.

When was the first film studio in California built?

a. in 1901   **b.** in 1911

Scan the passage quickly to check your answer.

Bollywood

Movies have changed a lot over the years. The movie **industry** has changed a lot, too. It has become much more **international**.

5 In the **early** days of **film**, most movies were made in the United States, near New York City. But the sun in California was **perfect** for filming. By the 1920s, most films, over 800 a year,
10 were shot in Hollywood.

Before films, Hollywood was a small town. There were a lot of farms nearby. The first film studio was built in 1911. In just fifteen years, 100,000 people
15 moved to Hollywood. Do you know the famous Hollywood sign? It was first used as an advertisement. A man who sold **land** put it up in 1923.

Hollywood was once the movie
20 **capital** of the world. But it isn't anymore. India is. Maybe you **recognize** the name Bollywood. Bollywood isn't a place exactly. It is a **nickname** for the film studios in Mumbai, India.
25 Why isn't it called Mollywood instead? The answer is that Mumbai used to be called Bombay. The movie business isn't **limited** to Mumbai. There are several other movie-making centers in India as
30 well.

A lot of people in India work in the film business—2.5 million. And the Indian film industry makes more than 800 films every year. Even Hollywood
35 studios send some of their work to India. Fewer than 500 movies a year are now made in the United States.

CHECK YOUR COMPREHENSION

Read the passage again and answer the questions. Circle your answers.

MAIN IDEA

1. What is the main topic of this passage?
   A. actors in the film industry
   B. places where movies are filmed
   C. Bollywood
   D. Hollywood

DETAIL

2. Where were the first movies made?
   A. California
   B. Bombay
   C. near Chicago
   D. near New York City

3. Hollywood became the center of film-making because of
   A. the farms
   B. the cost of land
   C. the weather
   D. the scenery

4. What does Bollywood refer to?
   A. New York City and Hollywood
   B. Bombay and Hollywood
   C. Mumbai and Bombay
   D. Bombay and India

INFERENCE

5. The Hollywood sign was put up
   A. because Hollywood was a famous place
   B. to help people recognize Hollywood
   C. to help sell land there
   D. because a man was proud of Hollywood

6. The Indian film industry
   A. is only in Mumbai
   B. is growing
   C. has always been large
   D. makes fewer films than Hollywood does

CHAPTER 3

Actress Sandra Bullock at the opening of a new movie

PREPARE TO READ

Discuss these questions.

1. Which film stars do you admire? Why?

2. Does the behavior of some stars surprise you? What stories have you heard?

WORD FOCUS

Match the words with their definitions.

A.

1. accept ___   **a.** repair
2. behave ___   **b.** agree to
3. control ___   **c.** act in the correct or proper way
4. downside ___   **d.** have power over somebody or something
5. fix ___   **e.** a disadvantage or the less positive side of something

B.

1. in public ___   **a.** possess
2. independence ___ **b.** have on your body
3. own ___   **c.** write your name on a contract to show you agree to it
4. sign ___   **d.** the state of being free or not controlled by someone
5. wear ___   **e.** when other people are present

SCAN

Guess if this is true or false. Circle *a* or *b*.

United Artists was called "the Home of the Stars."

a. True   **b.** False

Scan the passage quickly to check your answer.

Star-Making

In the early days of movies, the film studios made the stars. An actress like Carole Lombard **signed** a contract with a studio. The studio then **controlled**
5 everything about her life. The studio told her what movies to be in. It told her how to dress and how to **behave in public**. It controlled the actor's image. Sometimes, the studio even told an actor
10 who to marry!

Studios tried to "**own**" as many stars as possible. In the 1930s, MGM had 60 famous actors and actresses on contract, including Greta Garbo, Clark Gable, and
15 Judy Garland. MGM was called "The Home of the Stars."

So what did the actors get from the studio? They got a job, of course, and often a lot of money. Sometimes a star
20 got into trouble, and the studio helped **fix** the problem. Most actors **accepted** the control of the studios. There was no other way to work in movies. One group of actors wanted more control of their
25 films. Charlie Chaplin, Mary Pickford, and Douglas Fairbanks, Sr. started their own studio in 1919. It is called United Artists.

Today, actors don't give control of
30 their lives to the studios. Most work with many different studios. Russell Crowe can work for more than one studio. Gwyneth Paltrow can say no to a film. Jennifer Lopez can **wear** what
35 she likes and marry the man she wants. Of course, there is also a **downside** to this **independence**. Actors have to get themselves out of trouble!

CHECK YOUR COMPREHENSION

Read the passage again and answer the questions. Circle your answers.

MAIN IDEA
1. What is the main topic of the passage?
   A. the life of today's movie stars
   B. movie stars' bad public images
   C. the world's most famous movie stars
   D. how stars were made in the old studio system

DETAIL
2. How many famous actors and actresses did MGM have on contract in the 1930s?
   A. 50
   B. 60
   C. 70
   D. 80

3. Which of these is a downside for today's stars?
   A. making choices about what to wear
   B. saying no to a contract
   C. their independence
   D. having to get themselves out of trouble

4. Stars now
   A. must ask permission to marry
   B. control their own lives
   C. never get into trouble
   D. work for only one studio

INFERENCE
5. In the past, it was unusual for a studio to
   A. have 60 famous stars on contract
   B. control the lives of its stars
   C. have contracts with actors
   D. decide what movies stars would act in

6. Why did the stars let the studios control their lives?
   A. They liked it.
   B. They got a lot of money.
   C. They had no choice.
   D. They needed help to make decisions.

VOCABULARY REVIEW

From Chapter 1: *Carol Lombard: Actress*

1. What does *play* mean in this context?

> Gable played Rhett Butler in the movie *Gone with the Wind*.

  A. play *(verb)* to take part in a sport or game
  B. play *(noun)* a story written to be performed by actors
  C. play *(verb)* to act a part in a performance

From Chapter 2: *Bollywood*

2. What does *shot* mean in this context?

> By the 1920s, most films, over 800 a year, were shot in Hollywood.

  A. shot *(noun)* an attempt to do something
  B. shot *(verb, past tense)* moved quickly and suddenly in one direction
  C. shot *(verb, past tense)* made into a photograph or movie; filmed

From Chapter 3: *Star-Making*

3. What does *dress* mean in this context?

> It told her how to dress and how to behave in public.

  A. dress *(noun)* a piece of clothing worn by a girl or a woman
  B. dress *(verb)* to put clothes on
  C. dress *(noun)* clothes for men or women, especially for the evening

WRONG WORD

One word in each group does not fit. Circle the word.

1. studio	star	actor	actress
2. played	acted	lived	starred
3. land	town	sign	farms
4. dress	perfect	wear	clothes
5. limited	shot	filmed	made
6. film	capital	movies	studio

WORDS IN CONTEXT

Fill in the blanks with words from each box.

accident	land	make-up	owned	silent

1. There was no speaking in the first movies. The movies were _____.
2. Studios bought _____ from the farmers in California.
3. She wore a lot of _____ to hide the scar on her face.
4. The studios acted like they _____ the actors.
5. She was injured, but she was not killed in the _____.

contract	famous	give up	played	studios

6. It was difficult to find an acting job, but she did not _____.
7. The _____ give jobs to a lot of people.
8. *Gone with the Wind* is a _____ old movie.
9. He signed a _____ to act in three films.
10. Clark Gable _____ Rhett Butler in the movie.

capital	downside	limited	nickname	recognized

11. She became rich and famous. The _____ is that she can't go anywhere by herself any more.
12. His film name is Lorenzo, but most people call him by his _____, Buddy.
13. Everyone _____ her because she was famous.
14. Hollywood used to be the _____ of the movie industry.
15. Not everyone was invited to see the film. It was _____ to people at the studio.

WORD FAMILIES

Fill in the blanks with words from each box.

public (*noun*)	publicize (*verb*)	publicity (*noun*)

1. The studios told their actors how to behave in _____.
2. The studio will _____ the new film.

| actor *(noun)* | act *(verb)* | active *(adjective)* |

3. He was _____ in politics, but the studio didn't like that.

4. She is going to _____ in the studio's next movie.

| behavior *(noun)* | behave *(verb)* | well-behaved *(adjective)* |

5. How did the actor _____ at the party?

6. His _____ was terrible. The studio ended his contract.

WRAP IT UP

DISCUSS THE THEME

Read these questions. Discuss your answers with a partner.

1. What is your favorite old movie? Why did you like it?

2. Which of these statements do you agree with? Why?
   a. I would like to be a famous actor/actress.
   b. I wouldn't like to be a famous actor/actress.
   c. The old studio system was good for actors.
   d. The old studio system wasn't good for actors.
   e. Studios should not hire actors who get into trouble.
   f. Famous actors and actresses need to be good examples for their fans.

3. Where are the best movies made? Give some examples of good movies.

RESPOND IN WRITING

Look back at the unit and choose the passage you enjoyed the most. Read it again. Why is this passage interesting? Write a few sentences.

_____

_____

Now write one or two things you learned from the passage.

_____

_____

PSYCHOLOGY
THE MIND-BODY CONNECTION

▲ An exercise class

▲ A soccer game

BEFORE YOU READ

Answer these questions.

1. What is your favorite sport to play? What is your favorite sport to watch?

2. Which is more relaxing for you, playing sports or watching sports? Why?

3. How can exercising your body help relax your mind?

CHAPTER 1

Denise Austin at the White House

PREPARE TO READ

Discuss these questions.

1. Do you like to take exercise classes or follow exercise shows on TV? Why or why not?

2. Do you know about any fitness experts or celebrities? Who?

WORD FOCUS

Match the words with their definitions.

A.

1. active ___
2. advice ___
3. author ___
4. fitness ___
5. million ___

a. good physical health
b. 1,000,000
c. energetic
d. writer
e. a suggestion that someone gives to other people

B.

1. necessary ___
2. research ___
3. serious ___
4. skip ___
5. value ___

a. thoughtful; not joking
b. leave out
c. a careful study of something
d. importance
e. needed

SCAN

Guess if this is true or false. Circle *a* or *b*.

Denise Austin is a fitness expert and a businesswoman.

a. True   **b.** False

Scan the passage quickly to check your answer.

Denise Austin: Fitness Expert

Why should people make their bodies work hard when it isn't **necessary**? **Fitness** expert Denise Austin says that exercise is *more* important when life is
5 easy.

Austin is **serious** about good health. She is the **author** of eight books on fitness and health. She makes exercise videos. She also has two exercise shows
10 on television. **Millions** of people watch her shows and buy her books and DVDs.

Austin is also serious about children's fitness and health. **Research** shows that healthy, **active** children are also happy
15 children. Today's children watch TV and use the computer too much. Most children don't play outside or exercise enough. Austin made an exercise DVD just for children. It is called *Denise*
20 *Austin's Fit Kids*.

In 2002, the U.S. president asked Austin to join a special group. This group is called the President's Council on Physical Fitness and Sports. The
25 group includes famous athletes such as baseball player Nomar Garciaparra and runner Marion Jones. Some members are professional athletes or Olympic athletes. Other members are coaches.
30 Members of the group visit schools and talk to children about fitness. Austin teaches schoolchildren about the **value** of exercise and sports.

Fitness is not difficult. Austin tells
35 people to exercise a little every day and eat good foods. She follows this **advice**, too. She only exercises half an hour a day, and she never **skips** a meal!

CHECK YOUR COMPREHENSION

Read the passage again and answer the questions. Circle your answers.

MAIN IDEA

1. What is the main topic of the passage?
   A. the work of fitness experts
   B. the work of Denise Austin
   C. research about fitness
   D. fitness for schoolchildren

DETAIL

2. Denise Austin says that fitness is more important
   A. when you are a child
   B. when you watch exercise shows on TV
   C. when life is easy
   D. when you are a famous person

3. Fitness expert Denise Austin
   A. writes books
   B. makes DVDs
   C. has TV programs
   D. all of the above

4. What did the president ask Austin to do?
   A. join a special group
   B. use the computer
   C. make TV programs about fitness
   D. visit Olympic athletes

INFERENCE

5. When are kids happier?
   A. when they use the computer
   B. when athletes visit their schools
   C. when they are active
   D. when they skip meals

6. The president asked Austin to join a special group because
   A. she is an Olympic athlete
   B. she never skips a meal
   C. she is a famous fitness expert
   D. she likes to visit schools

CHAPTER 2

A bride and groom on their wedding day

Discuss these questions.

1. Look at the picture. Which person is the bride, and which is the groom?
2. Why do many people feel nervous before their wedding?

WORD FOCUS

Match the words with their definitions.

A.

1. army ___
2. celebrate ___
3. crash diet ___
4. last ___
5. lose ___

a. continue for a long time
b. have less of something
c. the military forces of a country
d. have fun on a special day
e. a food plan for losing weight very quickly

B.

1. model ___
2. panic ___
3. program ___
4. soldier ___
5. strict ___

a. a member of a military group
b. a good example to copy
c. very strong and unchanging
d. a sudden feeling of fear
e. a plan of activities

SCAN

Guess if this is true or false. Circle *a* or *b*.

Bridal boot camps are for soldiers in the army.

a. True   **b.** False

Scan the passage quickly to check your answer.

Bridal Boot Camp

For many people, their wedding is the most important day of their lives. Family and friends come, everyone **celebrates**, and people take a lot of pictures. Both
5 the bride and groom want to look their best. In the United States, some brides go to bridal boot camp to prepare for their big day!

Before their weddings, many women
10 feel the need to **lose** weight. Some women **panic** and go on **crash diets** to lose weight quickly. Some stop eating completely. This isn't good for the body, and the weight loss usually doesn't **last** a
15 long time.

Health clubs wanted to give women a healthy way to lose weight quickly and safely. So these health clubs developed a **program** just for brides and called it
20 "bridal boot camp."

Real "boot camp" is the training course for new **soldiers** in the **army**. Boot camp includes a **strict** exercise and diet program. The real boot camp for
25 soldiers usually lasts about ten weeks. Health clubs decided to use this **model** for their bridal boot camps.

Women in bridal boot camp meet at the health club every day for one to
30 three hours. They exercise, get advice about food, and help each other relax. They lose weight quickly but in a healthy way. They don't panic. When their wedding day arrives, these brides look
35 and feel better.

CHECK YOUR COMPREHENSION

Read the passage again and answer the questions. Circle your answers.

MAIN IDEA

1. What is the main topic of the passage?
   A. a special type of wedding
   B. a special type of exercise program
   C. a special type of bride and groom
   D. a special type of army

DETAIL

2. Before their wedding, some women
   A. join the army
   B. look at a lot of pictures
   C. go on crash diets
   D. develop a program just for brides

3. Women usually go to bridal boot camp
   A. before they get married
   B. after they get married
   C. before they join a health club
   D. after they take a lot of pictures

4. Bridal boot camps help women
   A. lose weight quickly
   B. stop eating completely
   C. go on crash diets
   D. celebrate with family and friends

INFERENCE

5. What does a bridal boot camp include?
   A. a strict diet
   B. a crash diet
   C. a wedding
   D. all of the above

6. Why do health clubs use the name "bridal boot camp"?
   A. because the brides wear boots to exercise
   B. because brides go away to camp for ten weeks
   C. because it is similar to army boot camp
   D. because it is for brides in the army

CHAPTER 3

◀ A yoga position

Discuss these questions.

1. What do you do to relax your body? What do you do to relax your mind?

2. What do you know about yoga?

WORD FOCUS

Match the words with their definitions.

A.

1. combine ___   **a.** thinking deeply and calmly for a period of time
2. competition ___   **b.** mix things together
3. demonstrate ___   **c.** have a different opinion
4. disagree ___   **d.** a contest in which people try to win something
5. meditation ___   **e.** show something or prove something

B.

1. mental ___   **a.** the way a person is holding his/her body
2. physical ___ **b.** need
3. position ___ **c.** about the body
4. practice ___ **d.** in the mind
5. require ___   **e.** do something regularly

SCAN

Guess if this is true or false. Circle *a* or *b*.

Today, many people do yoga for exercise.

a. True   **b.** False

Scan the passage quickly to check your answer.

Competition Yoga

Some people enjoy activities with a lot of movement, and some people enjoy calm activities. Those who **practice** yoga can enjoy both. Yoga **combines** the body
5 and the mind. It combines **physical** strength and **mental** relaxation.

Yoga is very old. It began in India more than 3,000 years ago. To practice yoga, a person first finds a quiet place.
10 Next, the person relaxes the mind through **meditation**. Then the person slowly moves the body into different **positions**. Many of these positions are quite difficult. The person holds these
15 positions for a long time.

Today, some people use yoga for exercise. There is even an international yoga **competition**. Yoga experts compete by holding difficult positions.
20 Competitors **demonstrate** their skill.

Not everyone likes the idea of competition yoga. They feel yoga should be relaxing. Competition is not a relaxing thing. Competition is about
25 being the best and winning.

People who do competition yoga **disagree**. In competition yoga, people don't compete against each other. They compete as individuals. They want
30 people to come to the competitions and learn about yoga. They want people to understand and practice yoga.

Yoga is relaxing, but it also **requires** skill. To be good at yoga, people must
35 practice it for a long time, like a sport. But is it a sport? Maybe both sides are right. What do you think?

CHECK YOUR COMPREHENSION

Read the passage again and answer the questions. Circle your answers.

MAIN IDEA

1. What is the main topic of the passage?
   A. the history of yoga
   B. yoga positions
   C. people who like yoga
   D. different ideas about yoga

DETAIL

2. What does yoga combine?
   A. strength and relaxation
   B. competition and exercise
   C. competition and sports
   D. relaxation and winning

3. A person who is doing yoga
   A. moves quickly
   B. goes to competitions
   C. holds positions for a long time
   D. must compete on a team

4. What is the big question about yoga today?
   A. Is yoga good for your body?
   B. Is yoga a relaxing activity?
   C. Is yoga a sport?
   D. Is yoga better in India?

INFERENCE

5. Why do some people dislike competition yoga?
   A. Competitions are only in the U.S.
   B. People must compete as individuals.
   C. Yoga isn't relaxing.
   D. Competition isn't relaxing.

6. Why do some people like the idea of competition yoga?
   A. They don't like other sports.
   B. It can help teach people about yoga.
   C. Competitions are popular.
   D. Yoga combines the mind and body.

VOCABULARY REVIEW

Complete the crossword using the clues.

ACROSS

4. Experts do _____ to answer important questions.

7. This is 1,000,000.

9. When two people have different opinions, they _____.

10. The writer of a book is called the _____.

DOWN

1. Something you want to copy because it's good.

2. People all over the world _____ yoga.

3. The military forces of a country.

5. People want to win first prize at a _____.

6. People _____ their birthdays with cake and ice cream.

8. If you must have something, it is _____.

WRONG WORD

One word in each group does not fit. Circle the word.

1. serious	funny	silly	laugh
2. teach	show	demonstrate	celebrate
3. sports	competition	exercise	model
4. panic	last	hold	stay
5. stand	sit	position	program
6. meditation	camp	army	soldier

WORDS IN CONTEXT

Fill in the blanks with words from each box.

requires	fitness	program	value	demonstrated

1. Bridal boot camp includes an exercise _____ .
2. Denise Austin visits schools. She teaches kids about the _____ of exercise.
3. The instructor _____ a new yoga position.
4. Yoga is like a sport because it _____ skill.
5. Denise Austin knows a lot about good health. She is a _____ expert.

active	combines	last	meditation	position

6. I like to do yoga because it _____ strength and relaxation.
7. When you lose weight very quickly, your results usually don't _____ for a long time.
8. To practice _____ , find a quiet place and relax your mind.
9. When you are in a chair, you are in a sitting _____ .
10. Some children spend too much time on the computer. They need to be more _____ .

mental	physical	serious	soldiers	strict

11. For some people, exercise is fun. For Denise Austin, it's _____ business.
12. I like activities that use my mind. _____ activities are the most enjoyable to me.
13. Riding a bicycle is a _____ activity. It is good exercise.
14. To lose a lot of weight, you must follow a _____ diet.
15. _____ in the army get their training in boot camp.

WORD FAMILIES

Fill in the blanks with words from each box.

loss *(noun)*	lose *(verb)*	loser *(noun)*

1. My sister and I had a competition. She was the winner, and I was the _____ .
2. The score of the soccer game was 5–0. It was a big _____ for the team.

| value *(noun)* | valuable *(adjective)* | value *(verb)* |

3. A wedding ring is very expensive. It is a _____ piece of jewelry.

4. She doesn't know the _____ of the ring. Her husband won't tell her how much it cost.

| advice *(noun)* | advisory *(adjective)* | advise *(verb)* |

5. The fitness instructor gave us some _____ about how often to exercise.

6. I wanted to lose weight, so I asked her to _____ me on my diet.

WRAP IT UP

DISCUSS THE THEME

Read these questions. Discuss your answers with a partner.

1. What types of physical activities (not sports) do you do in a normal week? Think of as many as you can and write them below.

<u>walk my dog</u>   _____   _____   _____

<u>carry groceries</u>   _____   _____   _____

2. Which of these activities do you enjoy? Put a check (✓) next to these activities.

RESPOND IN WRITING

Look back at the unit and choose the passage you enjoyed the most. Read it again. Why is this passage interesting? Write a few sentences.

_____

_____

_____

Now write one or two things you learned from the passage.

_____

_____

_____

UNIT 4

U.S. HISTORY
THE OLD WEST

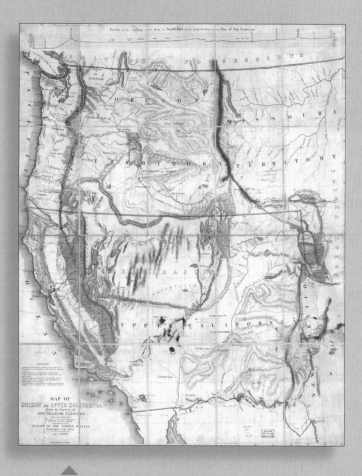

▲
A map of the West from the 1800s

BEFORE YOU READ

Answer these questions.

1. Look at the map. Describe what you see.

2. How did people travel around the United States 200 years ago?

3. How do people travel today?

CHAPTER 1

Charles E. Boles, 1829–1888

PREPARE TO READ

Discuss these questions.

1. Describe the man in the photo. Is this an old or a new photo? How do you know?

2. What do you think the man in the photo did for a living?

WORD FOCUS

Match the words with their definitions.

A.
1. bandit ___   **a.** a person in a book
2. character ___   **b.** a small piece of information
3. crime ___   **c.** go away leaving no signs
4. detail ___   **d.** a robber who carries a gun
5. disappear ___   **e.** an illegal action

B.
1. legend ___   **a.** a "car" pulled by horses
2. mystery ___   **b.** take something that belongs to someone else; steal
3. poem ___   **c.** something that is difficult to explain
4. rob ___   **d.** a piece of writing arranged in short lines
5. stagecoach ___   **e.** an old story

SCAN

Guess if this is true or false. Circle *a* or *b*.

Black Bart was a famous banker.

a. True   **b.** False

Scan the passage quickly to check your answer.

The Legend of Black Bart

Black Bart was a famous **bandit** during the 1800s. His story is a **legend** because no one knows all the **details** of his life.

5 People think Black Bart's real name was Charles E. Boles. Boles was probably born in New York around 1830. In 1849, Boles went to California to look for gold. During the U.S. Civil 10 War in the 1860s, he was in the army. Later, he got married and started a family, but he wasn't happy. He left his family and returned to California, where his life of **crime** began.

15 Boles was angry with Wells Fargo, a transportation company. No one knows why. He began to **rob** Wells Fargo **stagecoaches** in 1875. Boles wore a long coat and a sack over his head.

20 People began to call him Black Bart. The nickname Black Bart came from a **character** in a popular novel. The character was named Bartholomew, Bart for short. He dressed in black and 25 robbed Wells Fargo stagecoaches, just like the real bandit.

People called Black Bart the "gentleman bandit" because he was always polite to the people he robbed. 30 He was famous for this and for the **poems** he left at each robbery.

Black Bart robbed 30 stagecoaches in eight years. He stole over $48,000! The police finally caught him in 1883 35 and sent him to jail for four years. After he got out, he **disappeared**. No one knows what happened to him. His story remains a **mystery**.

CHECK YOUR COMPREHENSION

Read the passage again and answer the questions. Circle your answers.

MAIN IDEA
1. What is the main topic of the passage?
   A. a transportation company
   B. the Civil War
   C. California in the 1800s
   D. a famous bandit

DETAIL
2. Where was Black Bart probably from?
   A. California
   B. Illinois
   C. New York
   D. Wells Fargo

3. When did Black Bart first travel to California?
   A. 1830
   B. 1849
   C. 1877
   D. 1883

4. What did Black Bart wear when he robbed stagecoaches?
   A. a long coat and a sack
   B. an army uniform
   C. a black hat and gloves
   D. white pants and a mask

INFERENCE
5. What is true about Black Bart?
   A. He didn't like Wells Fargo.
   B. He didn't hurt the people he robbed.
   C. He stole a lot of money.
   D. all of the above

6. The end of the story is a mystery because
   A. Boles left his family
   B. Boles had a nickname
   C. no one knows where Boles went
   D. Boles wore a sack over his head

CHAPTER 2

◀ A miner looking for gold

Discuss these questions.

1. Describe the picture.

2. What would you do to get rich?

WORD FOCUS

Match the words with their definitions.

A.

1. announce ___   **a.** news or information that may not be true
2. discover ___   **b.** a person who looks for gold
3. miner ___   **c.** a large farm with horses or cows
4. ranch ___   **d.** tell everyone
5. rumor ___   **e.** find something new

B.

1. rush ___   **a.** travel on water in a ship or boat
2. sail ___   **b.** journey
3. search ___   **c.** something that no one else knows
4. secret ___   **d.** look for something
5. trip ___   **e.** go very quickly

SCAN

Guess if this is true or false. Circle *a* or *b*.

John Sutter was a rancher.

a. True   **b.** False

Scan the passage quickly to check your answer.

The California Gold Rush

In 1849, half a million people left their families to "**rush**" to California. Someone had **discovered** gold there, and everyone wanted to get rich quickly.

5　The story of the Gold Rush began ten years earlier when John Sutter left Switzerland. He traveled to California and started a **ranch**. A man named James Marshall worked for him. One day

10　in 1849, Marshall found gold in a river on Sutter's land. Sutter and Marshall kept the discovery a **secret**. They didn't want anyone to know about the gold. But soon people heard the **rumor**. Then

15　President James Polk **announced** the discovery.

People from America, Europe, and Asia rushed to California to **search** for gold. They were called the "forty-niners."

20　The **trip** took up to six months. It was long, difficult, and dangerous. Some people **sailed** around South America. Others traveled 2,000 miles across the United States by horse or on foot.

25　At first, there was a lot of gold. The **miners** found it easily. But by 1850, the gold was almost gone. It was hard work to find it. Soon, most people stopped searching for gold.

30　Most of the people who traveled to California never found gold. Some of the miners went home to their families. Others stayed and became farmers. Many sent for their families. Those

35　who stayed found something as good as gold—a new and better life in California.

CHECK YOUR COMPREHENSION

Read the passage again and answer the questions. Circle your answers.

MAIN IDEA

1. What is the main topic of the passage?
   A. the discovery of gold in California
   B. hard-working families
   C. miners
   D. traveling to the U.S.

DETAIL

2. Who first discovered gold in California?
   A. James Marshall
   B. John Sutter
   C. the "forty-niners"
   D. President James Polk

3. In what year was gold discovered?
   A. 1839
   B. 1849
   C. 1850
   D. 1893

4. The trip to California was **not**
   A. slow
   B. dangerous
   C. easy
   D. long

INFERENCE

5. Why were the people called "forty-niners"?
   A. Most of them were 49 years old.
   B. That was the year gold was discovered.
   C. That was the number of states.
   D. It took 49 days to travel to California.

6. People stopped looking for gold because
   A. it was too much work
   B. there wasn't much left
   C. they decided to do other things
   D. all of the above

CHAPTER 3

A recreation of a
Pony Express ride

PREPARE TO READ

Discuss these questions.

1. Look at the picture. What is the boy's occupation?

2. Have you ever ridden a horse? Did you like it? Why or why not?

WORD FOCUS

Match the words with their definitions.

A.
1. bravery ___   **a.** reliable
2. deliver ___   **b.** start a business
3. dependable ___   **c.** doing difficult things without fear
4. found ___   **d.** take something from one place to another
5. hire ___   **e.** give someone a job

B.
1. pony ___   **a.** physical power
2. strength ___   **b.** a machine that sends electronic messages by wire or radio
3. successful ___   **c.** a small horse
4. symbol ___   **d.** achieving what you want; making money
5. telegraph ___   **e.** something that represents something else

SCAN

Guess if this is true or false. Circle _a_ or _b_.

The Pony Express lasted more than 10 years.

a. True   **b.** False

Scan the passage quickly to check your answer.

The Pony Express

Most people can't imagine life without mail. Many of us get mail every day. Today, many of us get email over the Internet as well. But before 1860, there
5 was no **dependable** mail service across the United States. Letters took weeks or even months to arrive. Some letters never arrived.

In 1860, the **Pony** Express was
10 **founded**. The owners of the company wanted to **deliver** mail quickly. They used fast horses and **hired** boys under 18. The boys had to be small and very good riders. It was a dangerous job, and
15 the pay was only about $100 per month.

The Pony Express riders delivered mail on a route across the West. The route was 1,966 miles (3,145 km) long!

Each trip took ten days. The riders
20 worked in teams and changed horses often. The weather was often terrible, and the land was difficult to cross. But the mail arrived on time.

People liked the Pony Express, but
25 it ended in 1861. In that year, the **telegraph** was invented. The telegraph was a fast way to send information. Almost overnight, the Pony Express was no longer a **successful** business.

30 The Pony Express ended after only 18 months. But people respected the young boys who worked so hard to deliver mail. The Pony Express riders are **symbols** of **strength** and **bravery**. People still
35 remember what the boys of the Pony Express accomplished.

CHECK YOUR COMPREHENSION

Read the passage again and answer the questions. Circle your answers.

MAIN IDEA
1. What is the main topic of the passage?
   A. different kinds of horses
   B. the telegraph
   C. travel across the U.S.
   D. a special mail service

DETAIL
2. How long was the Pony Express route?
   A. 18 miles (29 km)
   B. 100 miles (160 km)
   C. 1,861 miles (2,978 km)
   D. 1,966 miles (3,145 km)

3. Why was the Pony Express founded?
   A. because it was dangerous
   B. to deliver mail quickly
   C. because young boys needed jobs
   D. to train boys to ride horses

4. To work for the Pony Express, the boys had to be
   A. farmers
   B. tall
   C. over 18
   D. good riders

INFERENCE
5. After their trips, the riders probably felt
   A. tired
   B. embarrassed
   C. jealous
   D. surprised

6. The boys changed horses often because
   A. the horses were tired
   B. they didn't own the horses
   C. the boys didn't like the horses
   D. they were bad horses

VOCABULARY REVIEW

Complete the crossword using the clues.

ACROSS

2. Find something.
4. An old story.
6. News that might or might not be true.
8. A small horse.
9. A car pulled by horses.

DOWN

1. Start a business.
3. A machine used to send messages.
5. Another word for a journey.
7. Someone who steals things.

One word in each group does not fit. Circle the word.

1. ship	boat	sail	ranch
2. legend	bandit	rumor	mystery
3. story	miner	poem	legend
4. dependable	bravery	pony	strength
5. bandit	crime	trip	rob
6. bravery	disappear	secret	search

WORDS IN CONTEXT

Fill in the blanks with words from each box.

delivered	get out	poem	search	secret

1. Black Bart was famous for leaving a _____ at each robbery.
2. The police need special permission to _____ your house.
3. Sutter kept the discovery of gold a _____. He didn't want anyone to know.
4. The mail carrier _____ the letters I sent to my friend.
5. Please _____ of my room now. I want to be alone.

bravery	miner	dependable	successful	symbol

6. The Pony Express riders were _____. They always delivered the mail on time.
7. Firefighters are known for their _____. They rush into burning buildings.
8. Bill Gates is very _____. His company makes billions of dollars.
9. My grandfather worked as a _____. His job was dirty and dangerous.
10. A flag is a _____ of a country.

announce	hire	ranch	rush	strength

11. I had to _____ to class. I missed the bus.
12. That big _____ in Texas has over 1,000 cows.
13. I believe the company should _____ me because I'm a good worker.
14. Did the teacher _____ that our final exam is on Friday?
15. Olympic athletes need a lot of physical _____ to win the gold medal.

WORD FAMILIES

Fill in the blanks with words from each box.

rob (verb)	robber (noun)	robbery (noun)

1. People who _____ banks should go to jail.
2. The _____ was a tall man wearing black clothes.

| announcement *(noun)* | announce *(verb)* | announcer *(noun)* |

3. The president was the first to _____ the discovery of gold.

4. After the president's _____, people rushed to search for gold.

| succeed *(verb)* | success *(noun)* | successful *(adjective)* |

5. _____ businesspeople make a lot of money.

6. You got an A on your test! Enjoy your _____!

WRAP IT UP

DISCUSS THE THEME

Read these questions. Discuss your answers with a partner.

1. Have you visited any Western states? What did you see?

2. Which Western states would you like to visit? Why?

3. Imagine living in the West in the 1800s. Describe your life. Where did you live? What job did you do?

4. How was life in the 1800s different from life now? Was it better or worse?

RESPOND IN WRITING

Look back at the unit and choose the passage you enjoyed the most. Read it again. Why is this passage interesting? Write a few sentences.

_____

_____

_____

Now write one or two things you learned from the passage.

_____

_____

_____

ANTHROPOLOGY
TOTEM POLES

Haida Totems, Cha-atl, Queen Charlotte Island by Emily Carr, 1912

BEFORE YOU READ

Answer these questions.

1. Look at the picture. Describe what you see.

2. Have you ever seen a totem pole before?

3. What do you think they are for?

CHAPTER 1

◀ Emily Carr, 1871–1945

PREPARE TO READ

Discuss these questions:

1. Emily Carr painted the picture on page 41. Do you like the painting? What do you like about it?

2. Why do you think Emily Carr's paintings are important?

WORD FOCUS

Match the words with their definitions.

A.

1. carve ___   **a.** something on paper or film that shows what happened
2. coast ___   **b.** a thick piece of wood from a tree
3. fir ___   **c.** land that is close to the water
4. log ___   **d.** cut wood to make an object or a design
5. record ___   **e.** a type of tree that is very straight

B.

1. repair ___   **a.** an animal or object that is a symbol
2. straight ___   **b.** fix or mend
3. totem ___   **c.** a wood pole with totems carved on it
4. totem pole ___   **d.** not curved or bent
5. village ___   **e.** a very small town

SCAN

Guess if this is true or false. Circle *a* or *b*.

Most of the totem poles that Carr painted are gone.

a. True   **b.** False

Scan the passage quickly to check your answer.

Emily Carr: Painter of Totem Poles

Emily Carr was an artist from British Columbia in Canada. She lived from 1871 to 1945. Carr studied the Haida, a group of Native Americans who lived
5 near the **coast** in British Columbia. The Haida **carved** beautiful **totem poles**. Carr's paintings are a **record** of these totem poles.

What is a totem pole? It is a wood
10 pole with large carvings called **totems**. The Haida used **fir** trees for the totem poles. These tall, **straight** trees grow in the Pacific Northwest. Haida artists carved the faces and bodies of special
15 animals on the big **logs**. Totems are symbols of a person, a family, or a **village**.

Each totem pole tells a story. Carr's paintings are important because these
20 wood totem poles only last about 100 years. Most of the totem poles that Carr painted are gone. The Haida didn't **repair** them. The wood totem poles were left to nature and the weather.
25 There is a lot of rain in the Northwest, and wood doesn't last very long.

Carr also wrote about life in the Haida villages. She described the totem poles and the meaning of the designs.
30 She explained the secret language of the totems.

Today Carr's paintings are all that remain of many of the totem poles. A special museum on Victoria Island near
35 Vancouver has many of her paintings. This artist left us an important record of Haida life.

CHECK YOUR COMPREHENSION

Read the passage again and answer the questions. Circle your answers.

MAIN IDEA
1. What is the main topic of the passage?
   A. how to carve
   B. the Pacific Northwest
   C. an artist
   D. a museum

DETAIL
2. When was Emily Carr born?
   A. 1871
   B. 1905
   C. 1945
   D. none of the above

3. Which of these statements describes Emily Carr?
   A. She was a painter.
   B. She was a writer.
   C. She studied the Haida.
   D. all of the above

4. What is special about her paintings?
   A. There are 100 of her paintings.
   B. They are a record of the totem poles.
   C. They only last 100 years.
   D. They all show the museum on Victoria Island.

INFERENCE
5. Which of these statements is true?
   A. The Haida used art to tell stories.
   B. Totem poles have no meaning.
   C. Emily Carr spoke a secret language.
   D. Most of Carr's paintings are gone.

6. What can we say about Emily Carr?
   A. She loved Haida totem poles.
   B. She traveled all over the world.
   C. She wrote about the museum in Vancouver.
   D. She didn't like to paint people.

CHAPTER 2

◀ Totem poles in Korea

Discuss these questions.

1. Look at the picture. Describe what you see.

2. What do you think these objects were used for?

WORD FOCUS

Match the words with their definitions.

A.

1. harvest ___   **a.** a force that brings good or bad things
2. luck ___   **b.** next to a road
3. pair ___   **c.** two things that are used together
4. protect ___   **d.** the amount and quality of a crop
5. roadside ___   **e.** keep someone or something safe

B.

1. signpost ___   **a.** a being that is not human
2. spirit ___   **b.** protect or take care of something
3. stranger ___   **c.** a person that you do not know
4. warning ___   **d.** a pole with a sign telling you where you are or where to go
5. watch over ___ **e.** something that tells you to be careful

SCAN

Guess if this is true or false. Circle *a* or *b*.

The upper part of the totem pole is always a spirit.

a. True   **b.** False

Scan the passage quickly to check your answer.

Jangseung: Totem Poles in Korea

In Korea, people place totem poles called *jangseung* outside their villages. The totem poles are meant to **protect** the village and keep bad **luck** away.
5 Farmers use totem poles to ask for a good **harvest**.

The Korean totem poles have big eyes to **watch over** the village. Many also have large teeth to protect the village.
10 Most totem poles are carved from wood. Sometimes the wood is painted. In the south of Korea, the *jangseung* are sometimes carved from stone.

Some of the *jangseung* are male.
15 Others are female. The upper part of the totem pole is a face. It can be a human or a **spirit**. The lower part of the totem pole has a written saying or **warning**.

Roadside totem poles in Korea are
20 found in **pairs**. One can sleep while the other watches the road for **strangers**. Some totem poles are used to warn people not to cut down trees. Other totem poles are **signposts**. They tell
25 people not to cross the land.

The name *jangseung* means "long life." It is very bad luck to damage a pole. One story tells about a man who used a totem pole to make a fire. Soon after
30 that the man died. People believe he died because he burned the totem pole.

Totem poles are important to many people in Korea. People believe the totem poles have the power to protect,
35 warn, and bring good harvests.

CHECK YOUR COMPREHENSION

Read the passage again and answer the questions. Circle your answers.

MAIN IDEA

1. What is the main topic of the passage?
   A. Korea
   B. a man with bad luck
   C. totem poles in Korea
   D. farmers

DETAIL

2. In Korea, totem poles
   A. are usually made of wood
   B. are always male
   C. never have eyes
   D. are in the center of the village

3. Why are roadside totem poles in pairs?
   A. One is made of wood, and one is made of stone.
   B. They are married.
   C. It is a government rule.
   D. One can sleep while the other watches for strangers.

4. A person who damages a totem pole will
   A. have a good harvest
   B. get very big eyes
   C. have bad luck
   D. become a totem pole

INFERENCE

5. Totem poles
   A. have only one meaning
   B. have many purposes
   C. are also made of metal
   D. are always found in large groups

6. What is true about totem poles in Korea?
   A. The stone totem poles are more important.
   B. They always bring a good harvest.
   C. They are symbols of bad luck.
   D. They can bring both good and bad things.

CHAPTER 3

◀ Typical animals on totem poles

Eagle   Beaver   Whale   Grizzly bear

PREPARE TO READ

Discuss these questions.

1. Describe the images above.

2. Can you name some animals that are symbols?

WORD FOCUS

Match the words with their definitions.

A.

1. adventure ___   **a.** be left after other people or things are gone
2. beaver ___   **b.** find and kill wild animals for food
3. hunt ___   **c.** an animal that cuts trees down with its teeth
4. region ___   **d.** an experience that is unusual, exciting, or dangerous
5. remain ___   **e.** a large area of a land

B.

1. represent ___   **a.** the soft part that you can move inside your mouth
2. similar ___   **b.** a very large animal that lives in the ocean
3. skilled ___   **c.** able to do something well
4. tongue ___   **d.** be a symbol of something
5. whale ___   **e.** mostly the same, but not completely

SCAN

Guess the answer. Circle *a* or *b*.

Animals were important to these people.

a. True   **b.** False

Scan the passage quickly to check your answer.

History Speaks: What Does a Totem Pole Say?

The most famous totem poles are from the Pacific Northwest. These tall wood poles with carvings once stood in villages along the coast from Alaska, 5 through British Columbia in Canada, down to Washington. Now the poles exist mainly in paintings and photographs.

Skilled artists carved the totem poles. The poles tell a story. The words of 10 the story are the faces and the animals, or totems. The animals sometimes **represent** the **adventures** of the village. For example, a carving of a whale may represent a very exciting or dangerous 15 **hunt** for **whales**.

You can understand the story when you look at the carvings. Birds and animals look **similar** on totem poles across the **region**. A face with very big 20 front teeth is a **beaver**. A face with a **tongue** is usually a bear. Whales and birds are also on the totem poles. These animals were all important to the people of the Pacific Northwest.

25 Wood doesn't last for long, so most of the old totem poles are gone. Some paintings and photographs of these old totem poles **remain** in museums.

Where else can you see totem poles? 30 There are totem poles in different parts of the world such as Korea and Polynesia. They look different from the ones in North America. But the totem poles all tell a story or represent a family. 35 They are a look at life in the past.

CHECK YOUR COMPREHENSION

Read the passage again and answer the questions. Circle your answers.

MAIN IDEA
1. What is the main topic of the passage?
   A. how to make wood carvings
   B. a description of totem poles
   C. a useful idea for big logs
   D. a tourist guide to the Northwest

DETAIL
2. Where were totem poles found?
   A. Alaska
   B. Canada
   C. Washington
   D. all of the above

3. The animals on the totem poles
   A. are always painted in bright colors
   B. don't have any special meaning
   C. are symbols that have a meaning
   D. are carved by the head of the village

4. Which of these animals is **not** discussed?
   A. a dog
   B. a bear
   C. a whale
   D. a bird

INFERENCE
5. The old totem poles are gone because
   A. they were in the Pacific Ocean
   B. they were outside
   C. the beavers, bears, and whales died
   D. people changed them every year

6. Which of the following statements is true?
   A. Carvings were similar in Alaska and Washington.
   B. Carvings of bears weren't found.
   C. People in Alaska also carved dogs on their totem poles.
   D. Everyone in the village carved totem poles.

VOCABULARY REVIEW

CROSSWORD PUZZLE

Complete the crossword using the clues.

ACROSS

4. An exciting experience.

5. Be left after others are gone.

6. An area that is close to the ocean.

8. A large area of land.

DOWN

1. A type of tree.

2. "Be careful!" is a _____ .

3. A person that you do not know.

7. The soft part inside the mouth.

WRONG WORD

One word in each group does not fit. Circle the word.

1. wood	log	fir	whale
2. protect	luck	guard	watch over
3. pair	danger	warn	curse
4. village	coast	town	city
5. carve	paint	protect	draw
6. harvest	food	farmer	stranger

WORDS IN CONTEXT

Fill in the blanks with words from each box.

beaver	pairs	skilled	stranger	tongue

1. On a totem pole, the animal that has big teeth is a _____.
2. The face with a _____ is usually a bear.
3. Some Korean totem poles are found in _____.
4. A _____ came into the room. We did not know his name.
5. _____ artists carved logs into totem poles.

log	luck	records	remain	straight

6. The man carved the face of a bear on the _____.
7. It was bad _____ to damage a Korean totem pole.
8. Native Americans did not keep written _____.
9. Totem poles are carved from tall _____ trees.
10. Some photographs _____ of the old totem poles.

adventures	harvest	carve	protect	similar

11. The animal carvings on the totem poles are _____.
12. Some totem poles told stories about exciting _____.
13. Artists _____ designs in logs to create totem poles.
14. The small _____ was not enough to feed the people in the village.
15. Korean people used totem poles to _____ their villages.

WORD FAMILIES

Fill in the blanks with words from each box.

represent *(verb)*	representation *(noun)*	representative *(adjective)*

1. The totems _____ different people or families in the village.
2. The animal on the totem pole is a good _____ of a whale.

| record *(noun)* | record *(verb)* | recording *(noun)* |

3. Carr's paintings are a _____ of many lost totem poles.

4. She tried to _____ the faces on the totem poles very carefully.

| adventure *(noun)* | adventurous *(adjective)* | adventurer *(noun)* |

5. They had a great _____ off the coast of Washington.

6. Are you an _____ person? Do you like danger and excitement?

WRAP IT UP

DISCUSS THE THEME

Read these questions. Discuss your answers with a partner.

1. Do you believe that objects bring good or bad luck? Why?

2. Do you have anything to bring you good luck? What is it? Where did you get this object? When did you get it?

3. What other objects do people use for good luck? For protection?

RESPOND IN WRITING

Look back at the unit and choose the passage you enjoyed the most. Read it again. Why is this passage interesting? Write a few sentences.

_____

_____

_____

Now write one or two things you learned from the passage.

_____

_____

_____

ARCHITECTURE
VISUAL ART

▲
Hearst Castle

BEFORE YOU READ

Answer these questions.

1. What buildings do you remember from your last vacation?

2. What is your favorite style of house? Why?

3. What can you understand about a person from his or her house?

CHAPTER 1

Julia Morgan, 1872–1957

PREPARE TO READ

Discuss these questions.

1. What is your favorite building? What do you like about it?

2. What famous architects do you know about?

WORD FOCUS

Match the words with their definitions.

A.

1. blend ___   **a.** make something again
2. design ___   **b.** a sudden, violent movement of the ground
3. earthquake ___   **c.** mix smoothly
4. natural ___   **d.** plan the appearance of something
5. rebuild ___   **e.** coming from the earth

B.

1. retire ___   **a.** admire; think about in a good way
2. respect ___   **b.** choosing when to do something
3. structure ___   **c.** stop working because of age
4. timing ___   **d.** about words and speaking
5. verbal ___   **e.** something that someone builds

SCAN

Guess if this is true or false. Circle *a* or *b*.

Julia Morgan worked on Hearst Castle for 28 years.

a. True   **b.** False

Scan the passage quickly to check your answer.

Julia Morgan: Architect

Julia Morgan loved buildings. During her career, she **designed** more than 700 **structures**. She was one of the best architects in the United States.

5 In 1902, few women went to college. Julia Morgan graduated with a degree in architecture in 1902. Then she got a job in San Francisco, her hometown. She was the first woman architect in 10 California.

Morgan liked to design "California-style" buildings. These buildings used local materials and **natural** colors. The buildings **blended** into the area.

15 In 1904, Morgan started her own business. She didn't know it, but her **timing** was perfect. In 1906, San Francisco had a terrible **earthquake** and fire. It destroyed many buildings.

20 People had to **rebuild** their shops, offices, and homes. Morgan was suddenly a very busy woman.

Morgan and her work were soon famous. People **respected** Morgan and 25 her ideas. In 1919, William Hearst hired Morgan to design his new house. He was a very rich and powerful man. He wanted to build a castle in San Simeon, California. This was a big job. Morgan 30 worked on Hearst Castle for 28 years.

Julia Morgan **retired** in 1951. Before she died in 1957, she burned many of her papers. She didn't want people to read about her buildings. She wanted 35 people to look at them. "Architecture," Julia Morgan said, "is a visual, not a **verbal** art."

CHECK YOUR COMPREHENSION

Read the passage again and answer the questions. Circle your answers.

MAIN IDEA

1. What is the main topic of the passage?
   A. a famous style of architecture
   B. a famous architect
   C. a famous house
   D. a famous earthquake

DETAIL

2. What happened in California in 1906?
   A. There was a terrible earthquake.
   B. Hearst hired Morgan to build his house.
   C. Morgan burned many of her papers.
   D. Morgan graduated in architecture.

3. What is part of "California style"?
   A. shops, offices, and homes
   B. local materials and natural colors
   C. rich and powerful men
   D. earthquakes and fires

4. What did Julia Morgan design?
   A. homes
   B. offices
   C. shops
   D. all of the above

INFERENCE

5. Why did Julia Morgan burn her papers?
   A. She wanted to design more structures.
   B. She wanted to use local materials.
   C. She wanted her buildings to blend in.
   D. She wanted her buildings to speak for her.

6. What is probably true about Julia Morgan?
   A. She was an unusual woman for her time.
   B. She was the only architect in San Francisco.
   C. She didn't like castles.
   D. She didn't use materials from the area.

CHAPTER 2

◀ Hearst Castle

PREPARE TO READ

Discuss these questions.

1. Describe the building in the photo.

2. What would it be like to live in a castle?

WORD FOCUS

Match the words with their definitions.

A.

1. antique ___   **a.** make something full
2. ceiling ___   **b.** a very old and valuable thing
3. collection ___   **c.** the place in a room where you make a fire
4. fill ___   **d.** the top of the inside of a room
5. fireplace ___   **e.** a group of objects

B.

1. imagine ___   **a.** belonging to a particular person or thing
2. own ___   **b.** separate something into different parts
3. take apart ___   **c.** a park with wild animals
4. tour ___   **d.** go on a visit of a place
5. zoo ___   **e.** form a picture or an idea in your mind

SCAN

Guess if this is true or false. Circle *a* or *b*.

Hearst filled his castle with new furniture and modern art.

a. True   **b.** False

Scan the passage quickly to check your answer.

Hearst Castle

What is your idea of a castle? What does it look like? Where is it? Most people don't **imagine** castles in the United States, but William Randolph
5 Hearst did. He built a castle at San Simeon in California. The castle has 56 bedrooms, 19 living rooms, two swimming pools, and a **zoo**!

The Hearst family was very rich.
10 When William was a boy, he and his mother went on many trips to Europe. She taught him about European art. They bought art and **antiques** for their family's **collection**. When he grew up,
15 Hearst remembered those trips. He remembered the beautiful castles. He wanted to build his **own** castle. He planned to **fill** it with art and antiques.

Hearst hired architect Julia Morgan to
20 design and build the castle. He bought art and antiques to fill it. He also bought some antique buildings. Workers **took apart** the buildings in Europe. Then they sent the pieces to California.
25 Morgan used the **ceilings**, **fireplaces**, and windows in the rooms at Hearst Castle.

Hearst and Morgan worked on the castle for 28 years. Hearst grew old and
30 became ill. In 1947, construction finally stopped. Hearst died in 1951 at the age of 88. In 1957, the Hearst family gave the castle to the state. Today it is a museum. Thousands of visitors come to
35 San Simeon every year to **tour** Hearst's American castle.

CHECK YOUR COMPREHENSION

Read the passage again and answer the questions. Circle your answers.

MAIN IDEA
1. What is the main topic of the passage?
   A. the life of William Randolph Hearst
   B. the story of Hearst's home
   C. Hearst's art collection
   D. castles in the United States

DETAIL
2. On their trips to Europe, Hearst and his mother
   A. built castles
   B. took classes in art
   C. bought art and antiques
   D. took apart buildings

3. In Hearst Castle there are
   A. pieces from other buildings
   B. art collections from around the world
   C. more than 75 rooms
   D. all of the above

4. How long did Hearst and Morgan work on Hearst Castle?
   A. 19 years
   B. 28 years
   C. 56 years
   D. 88 years

INFERENCE
5. Why did Hearst want to build a castle?
   A. He wanted a museum for visitors.
   B. He wanted a castle like the castles in Europe.
   C. He wanted to protect his family.
   D. He wanted to live in Europe, but it wasn't possible.

6. In 1947, construction stopped at Hearst Castle because
   A. Hearst was too ill to continue
   B. the castle was finished
   C. Hearst died
   D. Hearst didn't have any more art

CHAPTER 3

A decorative ceiling at Hearst Castle

Discuss these questions.

1. What kinds of antiques do you like?

2. Do you have any antiques? Do you use them, or are they only for decoration?

WORD FOCUS

Match the words with their definitions.

A.
1. cause ___   **a.** someone who receives a service
2. chimney ___   **b.** something added to make a thing more attractive
3. client ___   **c.** a hard substance used in construction
4. concrete ___   **d.** a place for smoke to leave a fireplace
5. decoration ___   **e.** make something else happen

B.
1. instead ___   **a.** in the place of something else
2. solution ___   **b.** about a physical building or its parts
3. solve ___   **c.** particular, not general
4. specific ___   **d.** find an answer to a problem
5. structural ___   **e.** an answer to a problem

SCAN

Guess if this is true or false. Circle *a* or *b*.

Hearst didn't care much about the design of Hearst Castle.

a. True   **b.** False

Scan the passage quickly to check your answer.

The Problem at Hearst Castle

The most difficult thing about building Hearst Castle was the **client**. William Randolph Hearst had strong ideas about the design of his castle. He
5   wanted to use **specific** pieces of art in specific rooms. But there was one problem. Hearst changed his mind again and again and again!

Julia Morgan was the architect of
10 Hearst Castle. She had to redesign and rebuild rooms to match her client's new ideas. Sometimes this **caused** big **structural** problems. Morgan was an expert in design *and* construction, so she
15 found ways to **solve** the problems.

In one room, Hearst wanted to use an antique ceiling from Spain. The Spanish ceiling was in hundreds of pieces. It wasn't possible to rebuild it.

20 Morgan thought of a good **solution**. She designed a **concrete** ceiling. Workers put the pieces of the Spanish ceiling into the wet concrete. The Spanish ceiling is really only **decoration**.

25 In another room, there was an antique fireplace. Hearst bought a bigger antique fireplace from France. He wanted to use it **instead**. Morgan put the French fireplace in the wall, but the fireplace
30 didn't meet the **chimney**. Morgan had to design and build a second chimney to meet the main chimney inside the walls.

Morgan's solutions almost always worked and Hearst was happy—but
35 only for a little while. Soon, he changed his mind again, and Morgan had new problems to solve.

CHECK YOUR COMPREHENSION

Read the passage again and answer the questions. Circle your answers.

MAIN IDEA

1. What is the main topic of the passage?
   A. some of the buildings at Hearst Castle
   B. some of the problems building Hearst Castle
   C. some of the workers at Hearst Castle
   D. some of the visitors to Hearst Castle

DETAIL

2. What was the most difficult thing about building Hearst Castle?
   A. the architect
   B. the fireplaces
   C. the client
   D. the art and antiques

3. When Hearst had new ideas, Morgan often had to
   A. buy more art and antiques
   B. hire new workers
   C. cause structural problems
   D. redesign and rebuild rooms

4. How did Morgan use the Spanish ceiling?
   A. She put it into a concrete ceiling.
   B. She redesigned and rebuilt the room.
   C. She wasn't able to use it.
   D. She used one piece.

INFERENCE

5. Why was Morgan a good architect for Hearst Castle?
   A. She knew a lot about art and antiques.
   B. She knew a lot about design and construction.
   C. She knew a lot about Hearst.
   D. She knew a lot about Spain and France.

6. Why didn't the French fireplace meet the chimney?
   A. It was a different size.
   B. The first fireplace was not from France.
   C. It was older.
   D. The first fireplace was an antique.

VOCABULARY REVIEW

Complete the crossword using the clues.

ACROSS

3. When you stop working because of age, you _____ .

5. Walls and floors are _____ parts of a building

6. Hearst had a big art _____ .

7. People stand near the _____ to get warm.

8. Architects make the _____ of a building.

DOWN

1. This is the opposite of *general*.

2. About words and speaking.

4. There was a terrible _____ in California in 1906.

5. Find an answer to a problem.

WRONG WORD

One word in each group does not fit. Circle the word.

1. create	rebuild	retire	plan
2. house	building	castle	fireplace
3. collection	structure	art	antiques
4. design	plans	ceilings	papers
5. solution	answer	timing	result
6. house	office	shop	zoo

WORDS IN CONTEXT

Fill in the blanks with words from each box.

caused	imagine	instead	natural	rebuild

1. Some of Hearst's ideas _____ big problems for the architect.

2. Hearst didn't want a normal house. He wanted a castle _____.

3. After the earthquake in 1906, people in San Francisco had to _____ their homes, shops, and offices.

4. Julia Morgan liked to _____ buildings in her head. Then she designed them on paper.

5. Some people prefer plastic or steel furniture. Others prefer _____ materials like wood.

clients	own	solution	tour	zoo

6. Visitors to Hearst Castle like the _____. They learn about the rooms and the art.

7. A store has customers. A professional person, like an architect, has _____.

8. For every problem at Hearst Castle, Morgan thought of a _____.

9. Some children share a bedroom, but some have their _____ rooms.

10. At Hearst Castle, there was a _____ with many interesting animals.

blended	ceilings	filled	take apart	timing

11. Workers had to _____ a building in Europe and send the pieces to California.

12. When you look up in Hearst Castle, you see many beautiful _____ in the rooms.

13. Morgan _____ many styles of architecture to design Hearst Castle.

14. He was not late and not early. His _____ was perfect.

15. Hearst _____ many of the rooms with art and antiques from Europe.

WORD FAMILIES

Fill in the blanks with words form each box.

collection *(noun)*	collect *(verb)*	collector *(noun)*

1. Some people like to _____ stamps or dolls or old books.

2. Letters from famous people can be valuable. A _____ looks for these letters in antique shops.

| retirement *(noun)* | retired *(adjective)* | retire *(verb)* |

3. In the United States, most people _____ at about age 65.

4. People save money for their _____ while they are working.

| imagination *(noun)* | imaginative *(adjective)* | imagine *(verb)* |

5. Architects must be _____ . They have to think of many different designs.

6. When you decorate your room, use your _____ . You don't want a boring room.

WRAP IT UP

DISCUSS THE THEME

Read these questions. Discuss your answers with a partner.

1. What rooms are in a house? Think of all the rooms that can possibly be in a house and write them on the lines.

kitchen _____   _____   _____   _____

_____   _____   _____   _____

2. What is your favorite room in a house? Why? Is this your favorite room in any house or in one specific house?

RESPOND IN WRITING

Look back at the unit and choose the passage you enjoyed the most. Read it again. Why is this passage interesting? Write a few sentences.

_____

_____

_____

Now write one or two things you learned from the passage.

_____

_____

_____

UNIT 7

NATURAL HISTORY
ANIMALS OF THE PAST

Models of dinosaurs

BEFORE YOU READ

Answer these questions.

1. What do you know about dinosaurs?

2. Have you ever seen dinosaur bones?

3. Where did you see them?

61

CHAPTER 1

Edward Cope,
1840–1897

Othniel Marsh,
1831–1899

PREPARE TO READ

Discuss these questions.

1. Why do people look for dinosaur bones?

2. Would you like to look for dinosaur bones? Why or why not?

WORD FOCUS

Match the words with their definitions.

A.

1. argue ___   **a.** damage something so badly you can no longer use it
2. bone ___   **b.** hidden in the ground
3. buried ___   **c.** disagree angrily
4. collect ___   **d.** one of the hard parts inside the body
5. destroy ___   **e.** gather a number of things over a period of time

B.

1. enemy ___   **a.** recognize or say what something is
2. fossil ___   **b.** a group of plants or animals that are similar to each other
3. identify ___   **c.** a person who hates and tries to harm somebody
4. site ___   **d.** what is left of a plant or animal from long ago
5. species ___   **e.** a place where something happened in the past

SCAN

Guess if this is true or false. Circle *a* or *b*.

Dinosaurs lived in the United States.

a. True   **b.** False

Scan the passage quickly to check your answer.

Marsh and Cope: The Bone Wars

Dinosaurs lived millions of years ago. In the 1800s, scientists found dinosaur **fossils** in the United States. Fossils are the **bones** of these animals. The bones
5 were **buried** in rock for a long time, and they became very hard.

Edward Cope and Othniel Marsh were two scientists who found many of the dinosaur fossils. These science
10 professors **collected** fossils and named new dinosaurs. They sent the fossils to museums and universities. Cope and Marsh were very successful in their search for fossils. Both men wanted to
15 find more fossils than anyone else. The two scientists worked together, but they often **argued**.

In 1877, dinosaur fossils were discovered in Colorado. Both Marsh
20 and Cope went to the **site** with teams of workers. Their teams dug up many new fossils. The two scientists **identified** the fossils and wrote about them.

There was a lot of competition
25 between the two men. Both men hoped to find new **species** or types of dinosaurs. At one point, Cope said that Marsh stole fossils from his site. Then Cope stole fossils from Marsh. Marsh
30 even **destroyed** one of his own sites because he didn't want Cope to find it. Their arguments became known as the "bone wars."

Both men discovered new species, but
35 Marsh found more than Cope. These men became **enemies**, but their "bone wars" led to exciting new discoveries.

CHECK YOUR COMPREHENSION

Read the passage again and answer the questions. Circle your answers.

MAIN IDEA

1. What is the main topic of the passage?
   A. dinosaurs in the United States
   B. where dinosaurs lived
   C. the search for fossils around the world
   D. the competition between two scientists

DETAIL

2. When did the men search for fossils?
   A. in the 1600s
   B. in the 1700s
   C. in the 1800s
   D. in the 1900s

3. Which things happened in the "bone wars"?
   A. Marsh stole fossils from Cope.
   B. Marsh and Cope argued.
   C. Cope stole fossils from Marsh.
   D. all of the above

4. What did Marsh and Cope want to do?
   A. work in a museum
   B. find more fossils than anyone else
   C. destroy dinosaur bones
   D. stay at home

INFERENCE

5. Why did scientists want to find dinosaur fossils?
   A. They were tired of collecting rocks.
   B. They wanted to have lots of workers.
   C. They wanted to learn about past life on earth.
   D. They wanted to travel to other places.

6. Marsh and Cope were both
   A. well-known professors of math
   B. very good friends with each other
   C. interested in a fossil site in California
   D. good at identifying dinosaur fossils

CHAPTER 2

◀ A large dinosaur skeleton

PREPARE TO READ

Discuss these questions.

1. When did dinosaurs live? Where did they live?

2. Why do some places have more dinosaur fossils than others?

WORD FOCUS

Match the words with their definitions.

A.
1. ancient ___   **a.** a large area of land with very little water
2. desert ___   **b.** a quantity of something on top of another thing
3. glimpse ___   **c.** a quick look at something or someone
4. layer ___   **d.** very old; from the distant past
5. mud ___   **e.** soft, very wet earth

B.
1. realize ___   **a.** an area of soft, very wet land
2. shore ___   **b.** know or understand that something is true
3. skeleton ___   **c.** land along the edge of an ocean, lake, or sea
4. source ___   **d.** all the bones of the body together
5. swamp ___   **e.** the place where something comes from

SCAN

Guess if this is true or false. Circle *a* or *b*.

Swamps are a good source of food for animals.

a. True   **b.** False

Scan the passage quickly to check your answer.

The Morrison Formation of Colorado

The first dinosaur fossils in the United States came from the Morrison Formation in Colorado. Scientists discovered dinosaur bones there in 1871.
5 Today scientists continue to dig up fossils at this rich site.

The first dinosaur bone from the site was 33 inches (82.5 cm) long. At first, fossil hunters thought the bone was a
10 tree branch. When they **realized** it was a bone, they dug it out carefully. In one place, fossil hunters found several bones from one dinosaur. Scientists later put the bones together. The bones formed
15 part of a dinosaur **skeleton**.

Today this area is a **desert**, but millions of years ago this was a huge **swamp**. It was on the **shore** of an **ancient** sea. The sea and the nearby

20 swamp were rich **sources** of food for the dinosaurs. Some species of dinosaurs ate other dinosaurs. Sometimes dinosaurs fell in the swamp and couldn't get out. **Layer** on layer of **mud** covered the dead
25 animals. Their bones remain as a record of ancient life.

The Morrison Formation has many types of fossils from the sea and the land. There are fossils of ancient sea
30 animals and plants as well as dinosaur bones.

A museum at the site shows what the dinosaurs looked like. It shows how the land looked millions of years ago.
35 Visitors can also tour some of the fossil sites. The Morrison Formation gives us a **glimpse** of life millions of years ago.

CHECK YOUR COMPREHENSION

Read the passage again and answer the questions. Circle your answers.

MAIN IDEA

1. What is the main topic of the passage?
   A. people who hunt for fossils
   B. a site where fossils are found
   C. life in an ancient sea
   D. a fossil museum

DETAIL

2. Millions of years ago the Morrison Formation was
   A. sea and swamp
   B. sea and desert
   C. desert and mountains
   D. desert and swamp

3. The first dinosaur bone found at the site
   A. was discovered in the water
   B. was only five inches long
   C. was found on the ground under a tree
   D. looked like a tree branch

4. The Morrison Formation has fossils of
   A. plants
   B. sea animals
   C. dinosaurs
   D. all of the above

INFERENCE

5. Which is true about the site?
   A. The climate changed from wet to dry.
   B. The climate stayed the same as it was before.
   C. The dinosaurs made the land dry out.
   D. Scientists dried out the land before they started to dig for bones.

6. Why did so many dinosaurs live there?
   A. It was a beautiful place.
   B. All of the rest of the land was desert.
   C. They were afraid to move.
   D. There was a lot of food and water.

CHAPTER 3

◀ A model of a mammoth

PREPARE TO READ

Discuss these questions.

1. Do scientists today still find fossils?

2. Are there any fossil sites near your town or city?

WORD FOCUS

Match the words with their definitions.

A.

1. bubble ___   **a.** very large
2. examine ___   **b.** outside a building, in the open air
3. giant ___   **c.** a substance for making or doing something
4. material ___   **d.** rise up because of air or gas trapped underneath
5. outdoors ___   **e.** look at something carefully

B.

1. pit ___   **a.** a thick black sticky liquid
2. remove ___   **b.** soft and difficult to remove
3. sticky ___   **c.** take something out
4. substance ___   **d.** a large hole in the ground
5. tar ___   **e.** a solid or liquid material

SCAN

Guess if this is true or false. Circle *a* or *b*.

Scientists allow people to watch as they clean the fossils.

a. True   **b.** False

Scan the passage quickly to check your answer.

Hunting for Fossils in Los Angeles

Hunting for fossils is usually done **outdoors**. In Los Angeles, at the La Brea **Tar Pits**, scientists work both inside and outside. The museum at the site has an
5 unusual room near one of the pits. Here scientists **examine** fossils of animals that are thousands of years old. Visitors can watch as scientists **remove** fossils from the tar. In another room, visitors can
10 watch scientists clean tar from the bones.

Since 1908, scientists have found more than one million fossils at La Brea. The fossils are from animals that walked around Los Angeles 10,000 to 40,000
15 years ago. This includes over 2,000 tiger skeletons. The species found at La Brea no longer exist, but they are not as old as the dinosaurs. The **giant** wolves, tigers,

and mammoths (a type of elephant) at
20 La Brea existed when the first people came to North America.

The "tar" in the La Brea Tar Pits is a natural **substance** called asphalt, the same black **material** used on streets and
25 driveways. Visitors can smell the hot tar and see it **bubble**.

Long ago, animals walked in the **sticky** tar and couldn't get out. Their bones became the fossils that scientists
30 are finding. Many skeletons are complete because the tar kept them in good condition. Scientists can study them and tell us about life in Los Angeles 40,000 years ago. Los Angeles has always had a
35 wild side.

CHECK YOUR COMPREHENSION

Read the passage again and answer the questions. Circle your answers.

MAIN IDEA
1. What is the main topic of the passage?
   A. what a tar pit looks like
   B. fossils from dinosaurs
   C. the tigers that lived long ago
   D. finding fossils in Los Angeles today

DETAIL
2. The La Brea Tar Pits still have
   A. animals falling into them
   B. bubbling tar
   C. active tigers in them
   D. dinosaurs

3. Which of the following did **not** live at the same time?
   A. dinosaurs
   B. tigers
   C. wolves
   D. people

4. How many fossils have scientists found in the La Brea Tar Pits?
   A. 2,000
   B. 10,000
   C. 40,000
   D. over one million

INFERENCE
5. Why do scientists allow visitors to watch?
   A. Visitors can learn about the past.
   B. The visitors can help clean the fossils.
   C. The visitors can watch for tigers.
   D. Scientists usually have people watch their work.

6. Which of the following statements is true?
   A. Tigers once lived in Los Angeles.
   B. Humans were in Los Angeles 10,000 years ago.
   C. The wolves were bigger than today.
   D. all of the above

VOCABULARY REVIEW

CROSSWORD PUZZLE

Complete the crossword using the clues.

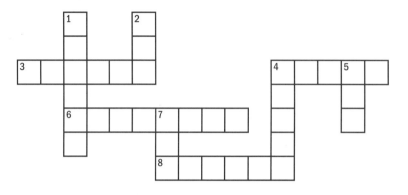

ACROSS

3. This is land with very little water.

4. This is an area of soft, very wet land.

6. Recognize or say what something is.

8. Take something out.

DOWN

1. The remains of a plant or animal from long ago.

2. A large hole in the ground.

4. This is land along the edge of an ocean, lake, or sea.

5. Soft, very wet earth.

7. A thick black sticky liquid.

WRONG WORD

One word in each group does not fit. Circle the word.

1. bones   fossils   skeletons   desert

2. glimpse   giant   huge   large

3. sea   swamp   bubble   shore

4. discover   destroy   uncover   find

5. site   location   place   examine

6. species   swamp   kind   type

WORDS IN CONTEXT

Fill in the blanks with words from each box.

bubbled	destroyed	fossils	identify	site

1. Marsh and Cope wanted to _____ new types of dinosaurs.
2. Tar _____ up from the ground. The smell was terrible.
3. Marsh _____ one of his own fossil sites.
4. _____ are very old remains of animals and plants.
5. The new _____ had a lot of dinosaur bones. It was a rich source of fossils.

ancient	desert	layers	realized	swamp

6. A _____ is very wet land. There are usually a lot of plants and animals.
7. The Morrison Formation is the site of an _____ sea.
8. Fossil hunters _____ that the tree branch was really a bone.
9. A _____ is a very dry place with few plants.
10. Many _____ of mud covered the dinosaur bones.

giant	outdoors	pit	removed	skeleton

11. Most fossil hunters work _____.
12. The dinosaur _____ is almost complete. Only a few bones are missing.
13. Scientists _____ the fossils from the tar pit.
14. _____ animals lived in the area that is now Los Angeles.
15. The tiger fell into the _____. It could not get out.

WORD FAMILIES

Fill in the blanks with words from each box.

argue *(verb)*	argument *(noun)*	argumentative *(adjective)*

1. Marsh and Cope used to _____ about everything.
2. The two scientists had an _____ over the name of a fossil.

identity *(noun)*	identify *(verb)*	identification *(noun)*

3. He is very good at plant _____ .

4. He can _____ every species correctly.

destruction *(noun)*	destroy *(verb)*	destructive *(adjective)*

5. Please dig carefully. We must not _____ the site.

6. The _____ of the site caused the loss of many fossils.

WRAP IT UP

DISCUSS THE THEME

Read these questions. Discuss your answers with a partner.

1. Why do people like to know about dinosaurs?

2. What can we learn from fossils?

3. Is this information important to our lives today?

4. Are there any animals today that look like dinosaurs?

5. Could dinosaurs live on the Earth today? If so, where?

6. Do you think that the dinosaurs in movies act like the real ones did? Why or why not?

RESPOND IN WRITING

Look back at the unit and choose the passage you enjoyed the most. Read it again. Why is this passage interesting? Write a few sentences.

_____

_____

_____

Now write one or two things you learned from the passage.

_____

_____

_____

TECHNOLOGY
COMPUTERS AND THE INTERNET

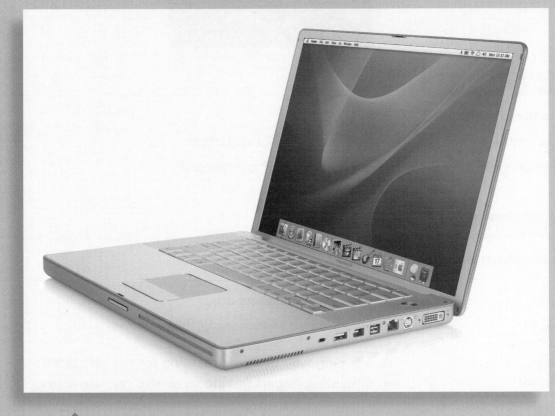

▲ A laptop computer

BEFORE YOU READ

Answer these questions.

1. Do you have a computer at home? What type of computer is it?

2. What do you use the computer for?

3. What do you know about the first home computer? Who made it?

CHAPTER 1

◀ Steve Jobs, 1955–

PREPARE TO READ

Discuss these questions.

1. Imagine life without computers. What would be different?
2. What do you know about Steve Jobs or Apple® computers?

WORD FOCUS

Match the words with their definitions.

A.
1. cr ive ___   **a.** liked more than any other
2. drop out ___   **b.** using skill or new ideas to make things
3. favorite ___   **c.** quit school
4. garage ___   **d.** a person who makes something for the first time
5. inventor ___   **e.** a building or part of a house where cars are kept

B.
1. personal computer ___   **a.** half a school year
2. popular ___   **b.** keep something for future use
3. salary ___   **c.** liked by many people
4. semester ___   **d.** the money that a person receives for work
5. store ___   **e.** a computer in a person's home

SCAN

Guess if this is true or false. Circle *a* or *b*.

The first home computer was built in a garage.

a. True   **b.** False

Scan the passage quickly to check your answer.

Steve Jobs: Modern Inventor

Steve Jobs, the **inventor** of the Apple® computer, worked for many years for a **salary** of $1 a year. Today he is one of the richest men in the world.

5　Jobs was born in Wisconsin and grew up in California. He was a good student, but he **dropped out** of college after just one **semester**. Jobs went home and joined a computer club. There, he met 10　Steve Wozniak. The two became friends. Both started working at a company that made computer games.

In 1976, Jobs and Wozniak built the first **personal computer**, the Apple®, 15　in a **garage**. The friends started their company Apple Computer. The next year, they built the very **popular** Apple II®. In 1984, they built the Macintosh®. Small pictures called "icons" helped 20　people use the computer. Jobs added a "mouse." The mouse made the computer easy to use. The two friends made millions of dollars with their computers.

In 1986, Jobs started a movie 25　company, Pixar. Pixar makes movies with computers. There are no actors, just drawings. Some of Pixar's best-known movies are *Toy Story* and *Finding Nemo*.

Now, Jobs works with other inventors 30　on useful things such as the iPod®. People can **store** their **favorite** songs on this tiny machine. Tony Fadell developed the iPod®. Then he sold his invention to Apple.

35　Steve Jobs is a **creative** man. He has a special ability to guess what people will like and what they will use. Millions of people own one of his inventions.

CHECK YOUR COMPREHENSION

Read the passage again and answer the questions. Circle your answers.

MAIN IDEA

1. What is the main topic of the passage?
   A. an inventor
   B. a movie company
   C. a computer company
   D. a new invention

DETAIL

2. How long did Steve Jobs go to college?
   A. one week
   B. one semester
   C. one year
   D. four years

3. Macintosh® was a popular computer because it was
   A. easy to use
   B. nice to look at
   C. cheap
   D. expensive

4. What does Pixar make?
   A. music
   B. computers
   C. screens
   D. movies

INFERENCE

5. What do we know about Steve Jobs?
   A. He liked college.
   B. He never watches movies.
   C. He likes to invent things.
   D. He doesn't listen to music.

6. Which of these statements is true about Steve Jobs?
   A. He invented the iPod®.
   B. He acted in movies.
   C. He made computers easy to use.
   D. He worked with Bill Gates.

CHAPTER 2

Bangalore, India

Discuss these questions.

1. Do you know where computers are made today?

2. What do you know about India?

WORD FOCUS

Match the words with their definitions.

A.

1. beautiful ___   **a.** the work done by an engineer, using math and science in practical ways

2. college ___   **b.** a place where flowers, trees, and plants grow

3. engineering ___   **c.** nice to look at

4. garden ___   **d.** a person who has completed studies at a college

5. graduate ___   **e.** a place where people study after high school

B.

1. healthy ___   **a.** a place or position

2. location ___   **b.** for all people

3. overseas ___   **c.** the material used to make computer chips

4. public ___   **d.** not sick

5. silicon ___   **e.** in another country across an ocean

SCAN

Guess if this is true or false. Circle *a* or *b*.

Bangalore is known for its public gardens.

a. True   **b.** False

Scan the passage quickly to check your answer.

The New Silicon Valley

The area near San Francisco, California is called **Silicon** Valley. It got this name because of the large number of computer companies there. At one
5 time, most of the world's computer companies were in California. Today, it is much cheaper to build computers **overseas**.

Many computer companies now have
10 offices in Bangalore, India. This area is called "the Silicon Valley of India." It has over 1,000 computer companies. There are also many **colleges** in the area. The computer companies hire **engineering**
15 **graduates**.

About 6 million people live in Bangalore. It is one of largest cities in India. This city is very old. It was founded in 1537. Bangalore is called the
20 "**Garden** City." There are many trees and flowers in the city. Also, there are many **public** gardens and parks. People can walk around and see **beautiful** colors everywhere.

25 The city is popular with companies because of the nice weather. People say that it is a very **healthy** city. It is never very cold or very hot, so people like to live there.

30 The city is growing, and college graduates can choose the job they want. They can also ask for more money. Now, some companies are looking for new **locations**. They want to open offices in
35 other places. Soon, a city in Pakistan or China may be "the 'New' New Silicon Valley."

CHECK YOUR COMPREHENSION

Read the passage again and answer the questions. Circle your answers.

MAIN IDEA
1. What is the main topic of the passage?
   A. Bangalore is an old and beautiful city.
   B. Graduates can find jobs in Bangalore.
   C. The old Silicon Valley is in California.
   D. There are many computer companies in Bangalore.

DETAIL
2. Why do computer companies make computers overseas?
   A. The weather is better.
   B. The cities are bigger.
   C. It is cheaper.
   D. There are more gardens and parks.

3. Bangalore is called the "Garden City" because
   A. the city is growing
   B. the city is very healthy
   C. the weather is always nice
   D. it has many gardens and parks

4. How many people live in Bangalore?
   A. 4 million
   B. 5 million
   C. 6 million
   D. 7 million

INFERENCE
5. What do we know about computer jobs in Bangalore?
   A. It is difficult to find work.
   B. There are a lot of jobs available.
   C. Most graduates leave the city.
   D. Few companies have offices there.

6. In the future,
   A. computer companies may open offices in cheaper places
   B. India will be ideal for computers
   C. companies will return to the U.S.
   D. the weather in Bangalore will get hotter

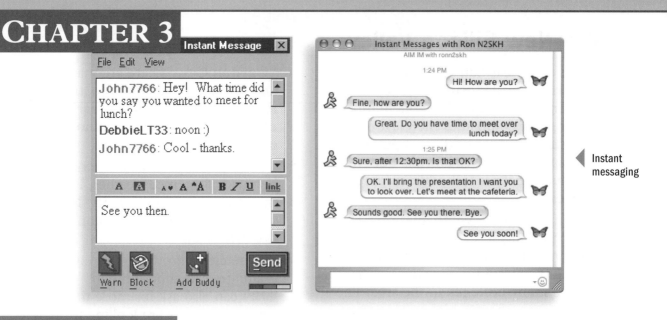

CHAPTER 3

Instant messaging

PREPARE TO READ

Discuss these questions.

1. What do you use the Internet for?

2. Have you ever used Instant Messaging?

WORD FOCUS

Match the words with their definitions.

A.

1. communicate ___   **a.** especially

2. connect ___   **b.** a very short period of time

3. create ___   **c.** join or link something

4. in particular ___   **d.** make something new

5. instant ___   **e.** give information to someone

B.

1. online ___   **a.** one of the 60 parts in a minute; a very short time

2. program ___   **b.** connected to the Internet by a computer

3. receive ___   **c.** a place on the Internet where people or businesses put information

4. second ___   **d.** instructions to make a computer do something

5. website ___   **e.** get something that someone sends you

SCAN

Guess if this is true or false. Circle *a* or *b*.

Email was invented by accident.

a. True   **b.** False

Scan the passage quickly to check your answer.

Technology Changes Our Lives

Computers changed life for all of us. Two computer inventions **in particular** changed the way we **communicate**: email and the World Wide Web.

Email, or electronic mail, allows us to send messages without paper or a stamp. In an **instant**, a person at a computer anywhere in the world can send and **receive** messages. Ray Tomlinson sent the first email in 1971. He worked for a company that was doing projects for the U.S. military. Their goal was to **create** a new way for people to communicate with each other.

The company created a network called ARPANET. Computer **programs** helped organize email on the network. Once only the military used email. Now anyone can send and receive email. Today, there are about 600 million email accounts.

The invention of this network led to the development of the World Wide Web. Tim Berners-Lee created the "Web" in 1990. It allows us to **connect** to people and businesses around the world. It lets us do things in **seconds** that used to take a long time. We can do research. We can shop **online**. We can go to different **websites** and compare prices. We can find maps and plan trips. We can buy airplane tickets or get hotel rooms without making a phone call.

Computers make our lives easier. Now, we can do almost anything without leaving our desks.

CHECK YOUR COMPREHENSION

Read the passage again and answer the questions. Circle your answers.

MAIN IDEA
1. What is the main topic of the passage?
   A. instant messaging
   B. shopping on the Internet
   C. changes in technology
   D. the importance of emails

DETAIL
2. Who sent the first email?
   A. the U.S. government
   B. Mark Arpanet
   C. Tim Berners-Lee
   D. Ray Tomlinson

3. What did Tim Berners-Lee create?
   A. ARPANET
   B. the World Wide Web
   C. the computer
   D. email accounts

4. When was the World Wide Web developed?
   A. 1960
   B. 1971
   C. 1990
   D. 1996

INFERENCE
5. Shopping online helps people
   A. find the cheapest price for something
   B. find the location of a store
   C. shop even when stores are closed
   D. all of the above

6. Email and the World Wide Web are similar because
   A. they both work on a computer network
   B. they were both invented for the military
   C. Ray Tomlinson invented both
   D. all of the above

VOCABULARY REVIEW

CROSSWORD PUZZLE

Complete the crossword using the clues.

ACROSS

1. A person who has completed his/her studies.

3. The material used to make computer chips.

5. In another country across an ocean is _____.

6. Something that many people like is _____.

8. When we join or link something, we _____ it.

9. Give information to someone.

DOWN

1. A place to put cars.

2. The work done by an engineer.

4. A place on the Internet where a person or business gives information.

7. Something that is available to everyone is _____.

WRONG WORD

One word in each group does not fit. Circle the word.

1. semester	college	overseas	university
2. graduate	communicate	email	connect
3. personal computer	online	public	website
4. popular	program	favorite	liked
5. house	garage	office	silicon
6. flowers	park	second	garden

WORDS IN CONTEXT

Fill in the blanks with words from each box.

garden	online	overseas	popular	seconds

1. I love to travel _____. Seeing different cultures is exciting.

2. People who look for things _____ are said to "surf the web."

3. The city of Boston has a large public _____ with beautiful flowers and trees.

4. Tom Cruise is a very _____ actor. He stars in many movies.

5. An email message arrives in _____.

connect	creative	garage	inventions	website

6. I just found a great new _____. It has cheap airline tickets.

7. He needs to clean his _____. He can't even park his car in there.

8. Inventors are very _____ people. They think of new ideas and new ways to do things.

9. Television is one of the great _____ of the 20th century.

10. To _____ to the World Wide Web, all you need is a computer.

healthy	instant	receive	salary	silicon

11. I _____ about 40 emails a day. I try to read all of them.

12. To stay _____, you should eat lots of green vegetables.

13. A good education will help you get a larger _____.

14. Computer chips are made from _____.

15. Computers allow us to do many things in an _____.

WORD FAMILIES

Fill in the blanks with words from each box.

invent *(verb)*	invention *(noun)*	inventive *(adjective)*

1. An _____ like the computer can change society.

2. A person must be very creative to _____ new technology.

| beauty *(noun)* | beautiful *(adjective)* | beautifully *(adverb)* |

3. She sings so _____. I love to listen to her.

4. Many people think Apple® computers are _____.

| create *(verb)* | creation *(noun)* | creative *(adjective)* |

5. She came up with a _____ solution for the problem.

6. The _____ of email changed the way people communicate with each other.

WRAP IT UP

DISCUSS THE THEME

Read these questions. Discuss your answers with a partner.

1. Do you use a computer? How often?

2. What do you do with the computer? Play games? Write papers? Listen to music? Send email? Shop?

3. Do you think computers changed our lives? Why or why not?

4. Are our lives better or worse with computers? Explain.

5. What will computers be able to do in the future?

RESPOND IN WRITING

Look back at the unit and choose the passage you enjoyed the most. Read it again. Why is this passage interesting? Write a few sentences.

_____

_____

_____

Now write one or two things you learned from the passage.

_____

_____

_____

WHAT TO DO BEFORE YOU READ

A.

1. *Possible answer*: A thin older woman is sitting outside; she's smiling; she's wearing a white shirt and a sweater over her shoulders. Her dark hair is pulled back in an old style. There is a hill behind her. It looks like a dry place. The painting is of a flower.

2. *Possible answer*: It seems to be an old photograph, and she is wearing old-fashioned clothes.

3. *Possible answer*: Maybe the passage will be about this woman and her paintings.

B.

1. The caption on the left tells us that her name is Georgia O'Keefe. It also has the dates 1887–1996. The caption on the right tells us the name of the painting, *Red Poppy 1971.*

2. She is no longer living. The first date is the year she was born; the second date is the year she died.

3. Answers will vary.

C.

1. The title names Georgia O'Keefe, so the passage is about a person.

2. Georgia O'Keefe is named in the title and is the person in the photograph. *Red Poppy 1971* is one of her paintings.

3. *Possible answer*: The passage will be about Georgia O'Keefe. She must be an artist.

D.

1. 10   **2.** 1

E.

1. The first paragraph

2. The last paragraph

WHAT TO DO WHILE YOU READ

A.

Does it have dialogue? <u>No</u>

Is it a story? <u>No</u>

Does it have technical vocabulary? <u>No</u>

Does it have charts and diagrams? <u>No</u>

Is it academic or professional? <u>No</u>

Does it have dates and events in a person's life? <u>Yes</u>

Is it a biography? <u>Yes</u>

B.

1. pioneer, portraits, countryside, landscapes, traditional, canvas, petals, skull, image, background

2. *notan*

3. 20th century, 1900s, 1986

4. 70 years, 98, hundreds

5. America(n), New Mexico

6. Georgia O'Keefe

C.

False. Georgia O'Keefe painted for 70 years, not for 98 years. She lived to age 98. (see lines 34–35)

> **TIP: Remember to decide what type of information to look for.**

D.

1. What is the main topic of the passage?

   A is not correct. This is just one type of painting. It is a detail.

   B is the correct answer.

   C is not correct. This is just one style of painting. It is a detail.

   D is not correct. This is too general. The passage is only about one artist.

E.

2. Women artists often painted

   A is not correct. *Children* are mentioned. This is one of the correct answers, but **B** and **C** are also correct.

   B is not correct. *Mothers* are mentioned. Mothers are women. This is one of the correct answers, but **A** and **C** are also correct.

   C is not correct. *Landscapes* are mentioned. This is one of the correct answers, but **A** and **B** are also correct.

   D is correct. This is the correct answer. It includes the information in **A**, **B**, and **C**.

   > **TIP: Don't choose the first answer that is correct. Read all of the choices.**

3. O'Keefe painted the desert of

   A is the correct answer. New Mexico has deserts. This state is mentioned.

   B is not correct. New York does not have deserts, and it is not mentioned.

   C is not correct. New Hampshire does not have deserts, and it is not mentioned.

   D is not correct. New Brunswick does not have deserts, and it is not mentioned.

   > **TIP: Eliminate any choices that you know are clearly wrong.**

4. What did O'Keefe paint?

   A is not correct. Trees are not mentioned. Butterflies are mentioned in a different way.

   B is the correct answer. O'Keefe painted large flowers, and she painted bones.

   C is not correct. Rivers and lakes are not mentioned.

   D is not correct. Other women artists painted mothers and babies, not O'Keefe.

   > **TIP: Sometimes a question combines details from two different places in the passage.**

F.

5. Which of the following is **not** true?

   A is not correct. People buy calendars, cards, prints, and posters. From this, we can infer that people like O'Keefe's work.

   B is not correct. O'Keefe lived to be 98 years old. That is a long life.

   C is not correct. From the description of the flower paintings, we can infer that they look real.

   D is the correct answer. O'Keefe studied *notan,* but we cannot infer that she taught classes. She was a student, not a teacher.

TIP: Be careful of words like *not.*

6. What can we say about O'Keefe?

   A is the correct answer. She painted natural things, and we can infer that she loved nature.

   B is not correct. The passage mentions a painting of a skull and sky but no flowers. The word *all* makes this inference incorrect even though O'Keefe did some desert paintings with flowers.

   C is not correct. She painted flowers and bones, but we cannot infer that she painted living animals.

   D is not correct. The passage mentions white bones and blue sky, so we cannot infer that she only used black and white paint.

TIP: Be careful of words like *all* or *only.*

G.

1. **A** In the early 1900s, many women artists <u>painted</u> **portraits**, often of <u>children</u> or of <u>mothers with young children</u>.

2. **A** You see the inside of the flower. You feel the <u>flower's soft</u> **petals**. You see <u>its bright colors</u>.

3. **C** One famous painting was the **skull** <u>of a cow</u>. You see <u>white bones</u> and the blue sky.

4. In the desert of New Mexico <u>everything is dry</u>.

5. You view the painting like a small insect, perhaps a <u>bee</u> or a <u>butterfly</u>.

6. You can feel how <u>dry</u>, how <u>arid</u>, the desert is.

7. O'Keefe studied *notan,* <u>a Japanese painting style</u>.

Vocabulary Index

A

accept **17**
accident **13**
active **23**
adventure **47**
advice **23**
ancient **65**
announce **35**
antique **55**
architecture **7**
argue **63**
army **25**
author **23**

B

bandit **33**
beautiful **75**
beaver **47**
behave **17**
blend **53**
bone **63**
booth **5**
bravery **37**
bubble **67**
buried **63**

C

capital **15**
carve **43**
cause **57**
ceiling **55**
celebrate **25**
character **33**
chimney **57**
client **57**
coast **43**
collect **63**
collection **55**
college **75**
combine **27**
communicate **77**
community **3**
competition **27**
concrete **57**
connect **77**
connected **3**
contract **13**

control **17**
copy **5**
counter **5**
crash diet **25**
create **77**
creative **73**
crime **33**
customer **5**

D

decoration **57**
deliver **37**
demonstrate **27**
dependable **37**
desert **65**
design **7, 53**
destroy **63**
detail **33**
diner **3**
disagree **27**
disappear **33**
discover **35**
downside **17**
drop out **73**

E

early **15**
earthquake **53**
efficient **7**
emotion **3**
empty **3**
enemy **63**
engineering **75**
examine **67**

F

famous **13**
favorite **73**
fill **55**
film **15**
fir **43**
fireplace **55**
fitness **23**
fix **17**
fossil **63**
found **37**

G

garage **73**
garden **75**
giant **67**
give up **13**
glimpse **65**
go out of business **7**
graduate **75**

H

harvest **45**
healthy **75**
hire **37**
hunt **47**

I

identify **63**
image **3**
imagine **55**
in particular **77**
in public **17**
independence **17**
industry **15**
instant **77**
instead **57**
international **15**
inventor **73**

K

keep on **13**

L

land **15**
last **25**
layer **65**
legend **33**
limited **15**
list **7**
lit up **3**
location **75**
log **43**
loneliness **3**
lose **25**
luck **45**

M

make-up 13
manufacturer 5
material 67
meditation 27
mental 27
million 23
miner 35
model 25
modern 7
mud 65
mystery 33

N

natural 53
necessary 23
nickname 15

O

online 77
outdoors 67
overseas 75
own 17, 55

P

pair 45
panic 25
perfect 15
personal computer 73
physical 27
pit 67
poem 33
pony 37
popular 73
popularity 5
position 27
practice 27
program 25, 77
protect 45
public 75

R

ranch 35
realist 3
realize 65
rebuild 53
receive 77
recognize 15

record 43
region 47
remain 47
remove 67
repair 43
represent 47
require 27
research 23
respect 53
retire 53
roadside 45
rob 33
rumor 35
rush 35

S

sail 35
salary 73
scar 13
search 35
second 77
secret 35
semester 73
sense 3
serious 23
serve 5
shore 65
sign 17
signpost 45
silent 13
silicon 75
similar 47
simple 5
site 63
skeleton 65
skilled 47
skip 23
sleek 7
soldier 25
solution 57
solve 57
source 65
species 63
specific 57
spirit 45
stagecoach 33
star 13
sticky 67

stool 5
store 73
straight 43
stranger 45
strength 37
strict 25
structural 57
structure 53
studio 13
substance 67
successful 37
surround 7
swamp 65
symbol 37

T

take apart 55
tar 67
tear down 7
telegraph 37
timing 53
tongue 47
totem 43
totem pole 43
tour 55
trendy 7
trip 35

V

value 23
verbal 53
village 43

W

wagon 5
warning 45
watch over 45
wear 17
website 77
whale 47

Z

zoo 5

COMMON IRREGULAR VERBS

INFINITIVE	SIMPLE PAST	PAST PARTICIPLE
be	was/were	been
become	became	become
begin	began	begun
blow	blew	blown
break	broke	broken
bring	brought	brought
build	built	built
buy	bought	bought
catch	caught	caught
choose	chose	chosen
come	came	come
cost	cost	cost
cut	cut	cut
do	did	done
draw	drew	drawn
drive	drove	driven
eat	ate	eaten
fall	fell	fallen
feel	felt	felt
find	found	found
fly	flew	flown
forget	forgot	forgotten
freeze	froze	frozen
get	got	gotten
give	gave	given
go	went	gone/been
grow	grew	grown
hang	hung	hung
have	had	had
hear	heard	heard
hold	held	held
hurt	hurt	hurt
keep	kept	kept
know	knew	known
lay	laid	laid
leave	left	left

INFINITIVE	SIMPLE PAST	PAST PARTICIPLE
let	let	let
light	lit/lighted	lit/lighted
lose	lost	lost
make	made	made
mean	meant	meant
meet	met	met
pay	paid	paid
put	put	put
read	read	read
ride	rode	ridden
ring	rang	rung
run	ran	run
say	said	said
see	saw	seen
sell	sold	sold
send	sent	sent
set	set	set
show	showed	shown
sing	sang	sung
sit	sat	sat
sleep	slept	slept
speak	spoke	spoken
spend	spent	spent
stand	stood	stood
steal	stole	stolen
swim	swam	swum
take	took	taken
teach	taught	taught
tear	tore	torn
tell	told	told
think	thought	thought
throw	threw	thrown
understand	understood	understood
wear	wore	worn
win	won	won
write	wrote	written